in the setting of administered prices. He tells us bluntly that a growing economy could not coexist with the kind of poverty which we have allowed. He asks what will happen to the precarious gains made by the Negroes in a society where piecemeal reform is no longer able to prevent the growth of an "under-class."

Professor Myrdal now directs the Institute for International Economic Studies in Stockholm. In recent years, he has headed UN economic studies of Europe and South Asia and later directed a study for the Twentieth Century Fund on development problems in South Asia. In this new work he addresses himself primarily to America. It is the kind of book that we have needed: eloquent and open, thorough and challenging. Once again, we are in Gunnar Myrdal's debt.

Also by GUNNAR MYRDAL

AN AMERICAN DILEMMA
The Negro Problem and Modern Democracy

BEYOND THE WELFARE STATE

AN INTERNATIONAL ECONOMY
Problems and Prospects

MONETARY EQUILIBRIUM

THE POLITICAL ELEMENT IN THE
DEVELOPMENT OF ECONOMIC THEORY

POPULATION, A PROBLEM FOR DEMOCRACY

RICH LANDS AND POOR

VALUE IN SOCIAL THEORY

CHALLENGE
TO AFFLUENCE

CHALLENGE

TO

AFFLUENCE

BY

GUNNAR MYRDAL

Professor of International Economics
at STOCKHOLM UNIVERSITY

NEW  YORK

Pantheon Books

A DIVISION OF RANDOM HOUSE

PERMISSIONS AND ACKNOWLEDGMENTS

THE AUTHOR wishes to thank the following
authors and publishers for permission to quote
from copyright material.

The American Scholar for "Trade and Aid,"
by Gunnar Myrdal.

Norman Thomas and *Harper's Magazine* for
"How Democratic Are Labor Unions?" by Norman Thomas.

Harper & Row, Publishers for excerpts from
*An International Economy: Problems and Pros-
pects,* and *An American Dilemma: The Negro
Problem and Modern Democracy* by Gunnar
Myrdal.

FIRST PRINTING

Library of Congress catalog card number: 63–19684

DESIGN BY HERBERT H. JOHNSON

Preface

FOR several years the sluggish and jerky development of the American economy has given reason for anxiety. A continuation of the present trend would increasingly frustrate the foreign policy of the United States. Internally the danger is that of clamping a class structure upon the nation in blunt denial of its most cherished ideals of liberty and equality of opportunity. The two dangers fortify each other in a cumulative process which threatens to move America away from that liberalism in thought and life that is not only the hope for a happy future of the American people itself but, as I have always held, the hope of humanity. I am inclined to feel that the most important problem in the world today is how to move the American economy out of the automatism of relative economic stagnation.

About these grave matters I shall speak my mind frankly. This seems to me the right thing for an economist to do whenever and wherever he makes a public appearance. He departs from his proper role and decreases his potential usefulness if he tries to be diplomatic.

Moreover, in this country I personally feel free to state my views bluntly and without any of the inhibitions of a foreigner, because I have come to know and love America so well through the accidents of life and work. More specifically, I find myself in complete agreement with the basic and traditional values which I once defined as the "American Creed," the radical ideals of the Enlightenment to which America has conservatively adhered. And I find these ideals to be so rooted in the American nation that in the long run they will be decisive in the development of policies, however many temporary and short-run aberrations may occur. But they must be constantly held up as beacons, particularly in the present era when history is accelerating and thereby increasing the danger that a convergence of such aberrations may cumulate and solidify them into a perverted and stale pattern in which the ideals could wither.

May I, at this point, be allowed to refer to my conviction that problems in the social sciences—not only the practical ones about what ought to be done, but also the theoretical problems of ascertaining the facts and the relations among facts—cannot be rationally posited except in terms of definite, concretized and explicit value premises.* The old and tenacious "welfare economics," which has been revived in recent decades, is in this view nothing but a metaphysical attempt at "objectification" of what cannot be objectified. In its very approach it represents a philosophical lag which hampers the adjustment of economics to the demands raised by events on the rapidly changing national and international scene. At the present time it is crucially important to bring valuations explicitly into social analysis and not to hide illogically behind the pretense of false objectivity.

This is the reason why, right at the start, I have brought up the American ideals of liberty and equality of opportunity. They determine both the viewpoint from which I observe reality and the practical conclusions I draw from my analysis. As values these ideals are not specific enough. When in this brief text I have had to abstain from stating my value premises more fully and concretely, I will meet that inadequacy by speaking in the first person singular.

The need for this is the more compelling because I know that my views are not shared by everybody, perhaps not even by the majority of economists in America, even though they, too, feel themselves to be in the great liberal

* *Value in Social Theory* (New York, Harper, 1958), and earlier works cited there.

tradition I referred to. This is so either because they perceive the facts to be different or because implicitly they apply different value premises. This is perfectly all right with me. I would, in fact, feel very awkward in surroundings where everybody shared my views. All this means that when I use the first person singular it is a *singularis modestis* and not *majestatis*.

The book is an amended and somewhat enlarged version of three McEnervey lectures on this topic I gave at the University of California at Berkeley, in April of this year. These lectures were in turn founded on a shorter paper I contributed to the Tenth Anniversary Convocation of the Fund for the Republic in New York in January. The piece on the West European Common Market in Chapter 10 is based on two lectures I gave, one to the Council on Foreign Relations in New York in January, and another to the Council on Foreign Affairs in San Francisco in April of this year. For some additional comments on the minority problem I refer to an address I gave in June 1962 at Howard University, Washington, D.C., published in *Race,* Vol. IV, No. 1, London, November 1962, and republished here as an appendix. I have largely retained the text as prepared for oral delivery.

While going over the manuscript for publication in book form I wondered whether I should remove from it references to earlier positions I have taken on the issues dealt with. In the end I decided to keep them in, and I want to state why I did so.

As the world changes and an author's experience and knowledge increases, it is, indeed, natural that he modifies his views on many specific points, and I am always happy when I find myself coming to new conclusions. On fundamental issues however, and particularly where basic ideals are strongly involved, consistency in views should be expected. On such issues it is natural that an author should feel compelled to think back upon positions he has taken earlier and that he should be reassured if he can see an unbroken line. In writing this book, it has been part of the candor I promised my readers to present my views as they really are: opinions, not hastily improvised at a particular juncture in world history, but held and expressed for a long time.

I offer no apologies for the rather frequent comparisons with Sweden, which after many years of work abroad I now observe again with fresh, somewhat critical, but sympathetic eyes. The comparisons, are, I believe, justified. These two spiritual fatherlands of mine, in spite of the difference in size, are more similar than any two countries I can think of, not only in the levels of consumption and production which they have achieved, but more basically in social and economic values. These include, incidentally, some I should like to see modified: for instance, the absorbing interest in plumbing and other traces of materialistic "Babbitism" in both countries and a creeping tendency to conformity in views—though in Sweden, contrary to the United States, conformity is more developed in the democratized and widely ramifying "top side" than among the masses of ordinary people.

I have had aid in preparing the manuscript of this book by critical comments from many friends and colleagues scattered in different continents who read the shorter paper mentioned above, and from some who also read a draft of the manuscript of the book.

THE INSTITUTE FOR INTERNATIONAL ECONOMIC STUDIES,
STOCKHOLM UNIVERSITY, MAY 1963

Contents

PART I

Relative
Economic Stagnation
in America

CHAPTER I

Survey of the Problems

Slow and Unsteady Economic Growth

THE record of economic development in the United States is unsatisfactory. When all is added up, the average annual growth rate during the decade up to 1962 comes out well below 3 per cent. The American economy seems to have settled down to a sequence of recessions, short-lived and inadequate upturns, and periods of stagnation in between. If there is any consistent pattern in the postwar era it is that the recoveries after the recessions tend to become ever more hesitant and to result in an ever more incomplete employment of the labor force in proportion to the rise in output. I have seen no evidence that would render it probable that the American economy by itself— *i.e.*, as a result of the forces now at work in that economy, including government policies currently to be anticipated —would get out of this rut.

This picture of the American economy is not a startlingly new one. Recent development corresponds fairly well to the general pattern of economic development in the United States from the beginning of the century and even earlier. In peacetime, the American economy has never expanded very rapidly, when we take into consideration the huge stream of immigrants, mostly of work-

ing age, right up till the First World War. And its growth
has always been a jumpy and unpredictable one. And
such was the pattern in the whole industrialized Western
world until the end of the Second World War.

But after that war not only the U.S.S.R. and the other
Communist countries in Europe, but also most Western
countries and Japan have had a rapid and fairly steady
growth—with the major and sad exception of Great Britain which, particularly in the last decade, has also lagged
behind in economic development. As has been thoroughly
analyzed—for instance in the yearly surveys published
by the United Nations Economic Commission for Europe
since 1948—this new pattern of development in most
Western countries after the Second World War has its
main explanation in a much more intelligent and watch-
ful economic policy on the part of the governments, even
if there are exceptions and even if in all these countries
great improvements are still possible and desirable.

The complaint that can be raised against the United
States, therefore, is that it has lagged in applying the new
knowledge we have about how to induce economic progress, and the new determination we have acquired to use
this knowledge to our advantage. And as we shall show
in this book, this unfortunate backwardness in American
economic policy has serious effects not only for the welfare of large sections of its own people but also for both
the direction and effectiveness of its foreign policy.

In the United States, the famous built-in stabilizers,
which came into existence without being designed as economic policies but nevertheless are bound to have economic effects, have, until now, prevented the recessions
from developing into serious depressions. But such a possibility cannot be altogether excluded. The supposition
that a depression, if it started, would not be permitted to
develop into anything like the Great Depression of the
thirties but would this time call forth vigorous government action, should not satisfy us. Policies should be ap-

plied ahead of time to make sure that such a depression could not even have a beginning.

Or rather, even assuming that the recessions will remain mild, since the whole established pattern of development is unsatisfactory, government policies should now be planned and executed with a view to pushing the economy into an entirely new pattern. The point to stress at the present juncture is that even a prolonged "boomlet" is not enough to accomplish this. The goal must be such fundamental changes in the conditions under which the American economy develops that the result is not only economic growth which is rapid for a few years, but is, at the same time, reliably steady in future years. Recessions are unnecessary in a properly governed country, particularly a big one that for this reason should be less dependent on what happens in the rest of the world.

When we discuss development in underdeveloped countries we are accustomed to thinking of growth in terms of the rise in national output per head. But when, instead, we measure the rate of growth in the United States, the U.S.S.R., the Western European countries and those in the other industrialized regions, we are usually less strict and calculate our economic growth quite simply in terms of the increase in national output. The failure to take population growth into the calculation of the rate of economic progress is particularly important for the United States, where the annual population increase is around 1.7 per cent, a fairly high rate for a rich country. In international comparisons, for instance with countries in Western Europe, the difference in the growth rate is thus understated.

If we deflate Western growth rates in the way we are accustomed to doing for underdeveloped countries, the figure for the United States for the decade up to 1962 comes out at around 1 per cent, not significantly different from what we believe—on a very rough statistical basis— the growth rate of poor India to have been for the corresponding period.

Consequences for Employment of the Labor Force

An ominous fact in America is the high and rising level of unemployment. The relative economic stagnation is not simply a situation where the American people enjoy such an advantage in current consumption and leisure from a high productivity economy that too little is left for saving and investment to keep the economy growing quickly.

In spite of the fact that its net investment ratio is nearly twice as high as that of the United States, this could perhaps be said about Sweden, which is almost as rich* and remains satisfied with a growth rate per head only about three times higher than America's. Sweden could, of course, save and invest more in order to raise its rate of growth. But at least it keeps up full employment and uses its other productive resources nearly to their full capacity. And it sees to it that *all* its people increasingly share the fruits of economic progress by enjoying rising standards of consumption and planned leisure.

Sweden's policies can thus be criticized—and are being criticized—from the point of view that it ought to restrain consumption further to permit a still higher level of investment and a higher growth rate. Or, as is argued by others, Sweden should perfect its economic policies even more, so that a higher growth rate might be realized which could then make possible still higher levels of both

* This statement is based upon many considerations, among them that in the conventional statistics on national output per head items of the production of services for collective consumption become seriously underestimated. In addition to this, fewer or less well organized public services in many ways imply disutilities and additional costs which should be taken into account.

consumption and investment, even without an initial sacrifice on the part of the consumers. It has been pointed out that the traditional national accounting concepts of saving and investment are unrealistic and that a still greater share of the national product devoted to education, research, and other forms of public consumption might be more conducive to raising the rate of economic growth than more physical investment.

Without entering upon a discussion of how a higher growth rate could be achieved, it should be stated that this criticism cannot be thrown aside lightly in view of the unsatisfied needs of the less privileged groups that still remain even in the Swedish welfare state, not to speak of the abject misery in the underdeveloped countries. But, at least, the whole labor force is steadily at work, and what is invested is being used fully and fairly effectively.

This is not the case in America. What is most disastrous for the national welfare and, as can be feared, in the end for national unity, is that while part of the American people live in affluence—sometimes a rather vulgar affluence of satisfying needs created by high-pressure advertising, in conflict with the inherited Puritan ideals of high thinking and prudent living—a large, though mostly silent, minority enjoys neither security nor a decent standard of living. The thesis of this book is that it will not prove possible to change over the American economy to rapid and steady growth and full employment without taking vigorous measures within the American nation to induce greater equality of opportunity and of standards of living. Even if we should succeed in meeting the crying need for more material goods on the part of the poor, there are tremendous unfilled needs in America of more effectively constructed and organized communities, of human care of the incomplete families, the sick and the invalid, the old and the children and youth, and of higher culture in the whole nation. The creeping complacency that America is now an affluent society and has reached the levels of production and consumption that allows it to slow

down its economic progress is patently wrong. Add to this
that all of the rich countries are islands in an ocean of
underdeveloped countries where people live in a poverty
so abject and miserable that we can hardly grasp it as a
fact.

Besides, unemployment is damaging for the individuals
and their families. As it is rising, it is now on the verge
of stratifying a substratum of hopeless and miserable
people, detached from the nation at large.

Other Aggravating Elements in the American Situation

Another and equally ominous fact is that the sluggish
and jerky development of the American economy and its
increasing inability to give full employment to its labor
force has occurred while there has been "pump-priming"
of a truly extraordinary magnitude in the form of huge
expenditures for national defense. These expenditures—
including the billions for adventures in space—swallow
up half of the increasing national budget, or about 10 per
cent of the gross national product. They are bigger than
America's total fixed business investment and correspond
to more than two thirds of all private domestic investments. The armed forces employ considerably more than
half as many as the unemployed in the civilian labor
force, who are very many.

That in the present international situation these expenditures and this employment of a large part of the
labor force are deemed to be politically necessary—which
in the present context I shall not question—does not in
the slightest detract from the serious observation an
economist must make: that the growth of the American
economy seems remarkably unsatisfactory and the un-

employment figures particularly high when we realize that it depends upon this tremendous pump-priming of huge and, in absolute terms, rising armament expenditures. The need to undertake these expenditures and to use such a large part of the labor force in this way would have put a healthy economy under strain. As we have seen, the American economy, on the contrary, finds it ever more difficult to employ its labor force and to use its resources, *in spite of* this extraordinary demand for producing products and services not entering as supplies in the markets.

Another aggravating element in the American situation is the deterioration of the United States international exchange position. Within the last decade the foreign exchange situation has changed radically in a way unfavorable to the United States. Instead of the world dollar shortage characterizing the first decade after the war, the United States has now for a number of years felt increasing difficulty in meeting its various military and civilian commitments abroad out of its export surplus and in allowing for the private investments and capital outflow that occur. The result has been a decrease of its gold holdings and, even more importantly, an increase of its liquid liabilities, putting the American economy at the mercy of forces abroad which its government does not control—at least as long as its growth rate is not more rapid and without taking specific policy measures having no other motivation than that they are needed to defend the exchange balance.

The relation of this development on the foreign exchange front to the unsatisfactory economic development at home is twofold. On the one hand, as is generally recognized, the uncomfortable exchange situation has caused the American government to apply constraints on the domestic money and capital market which have tended to keep down demand and investment at home. It has, in any case, caused the government to hesitate in taking action to stimulate business in America, lest this should lead to a decrease of the export surplus and at the same time create adverse expectations at home and abroad that would lead to an increased net capital outflow; both effects feared as leading to a further deterioration of the United States exchange situation. The foreign exchange situation today remains in the economic debate in the United States a consideration that makes most people hesitant to go in for an expansionist policy.

On the other hand, there is no doubt that in many ways the lack of vigorous expansion of the American economy has itself decreased its competitive strength in both the international commodity and capital markets. The countries which in recent years have strengthened their international exchange situation at the expense of the United States have all had a high growth rate and a full or a rapidly increasing employment of their labor force.

Outline of the Argument

In the first part of this book we shall discuss the economic and social consequences at home of the slow and unsteady growth of production in the United States. We will start out by a consideration of the high and rising level of unemployment and of the causes of this trend. This will bring us to the wider problem of poverty in the midst of plenty and of the operation of a vicious circle tending to create in America an unprivileged class of unemployed, unemployables, and underemployed who are more and more hopelessly set apart from the nation at large and do not share in its life, its ambitions, and its achievements.

As this unutilized or underutilized substratum of the American people at the same time represents America's greatest waste of productive resources, we will find that at this juncture of history there is a striking convergence between the American ideals of liberty and equality of opportunity on the one hand, and of economic progress on the other. Indeed, the chief policy means of spurring economic progress will have to be huge reforms that are in the interest of social justice.

To establish a new pattern of rapid and steady economic growth will necessitate much more co-ordination of policies and of national planning. And a full employment policy must contain adequate measures to stabilize the cost and price structure and to protect the balance of foreign exchange. These more technical problems will be taken up in separate chapters.

Until that point the argument can proceed on the level of logical reasoning from the known facts and the equally known and real ideals implied in the American Creed. To carry this argument and spell out the policy conclusions is the primary task of the economist. But it would be unrealistic to also avoid considering the opportunities for translating the policy conclusions into practical action, and the inhibitions against doing it that are present in the political attitudes and institutions of America. The last chapter of Part I is devoted to this problem.

In Part II the implications for United States foreign policy of the relative economic stagnation at home will be studied. Their general character is frustration—frustration of the United States' actual possibilities for influencing the outside world in the direction of its ideals and interests and, as a consequence, frustration also in the minds of its people. This latter effect of America's tardy and uneven economic growth is bound to be the more serious as the development of the whole world must give rise to deep feelings of disappointment and even fear in a basically peace-loving people, like the American, whose ambitions and hopes remain the civilian values of a good life for itself and all humanity.

CHAPTER 2

Unemployment

High and Rising Unemployment Rate

FULL-time unemployment in the United States now fluctuates around a level of 6 per cent of the civilian labor force: *i.e.*, excluding the almost 4 per cent of the total labor force who are in the armed forces.

Even in a country like the United States with a rather highly organized labor market and with an excellent statistical service, unemployment is a somewhat vague concept that both includes persons who should not be included and—still more often—excludes others who should be counted in. In the present context we need not enter upon these problems as, for our purpose, what matters is only the broad dimension of existing unemployment in the United States.

Only one technical point should be mentioned. It had earlier been held that the American unemployment figures implied a serious overestimate compared with the figures quoted in Western Europe because of the different ways of arriving at them. More recent official investigations have shown this to be less important than previously assumed or, as in comparisons with Western Germany and Italy, to have the opposite effect of an overestimate of the relative unemployment in those countries.

The figure for the unemployed must be increased by

an unknown number to account for two other categories whose idleness is not voluntary: those working part time, and those potential workers who under conditions of full employment would seek work but who do not now attempt actively to do so since jobs are not available.

Since the civilian labor force is above 72 million, the full-time unemployed are around 4 million—taking 6 per cent to be an average level for the time being. The other two categories afflicted by unemployment would, if their worklessness were translated into full-time unemployment, perhaps amount to half again as many, making the real unemployment equal to some 6 million workers, or nearly 9 per cent of the civilian labor force.

Spreading out unemployment by short working hours may in the present situation be reckoned as an improvement from one point of view. But it should be remembered that part-time employment means that more workers are afflicted with the curse of unemployment.

When workers, particularly married women and both men and women above the age forty to fifty, where they become less attractive to the employers, now begin to abstain from seeking employment, this inaugurates a different pattern of life and work in society. As such a situation in a period of prolonged and widespread unemployment comes to be felt to be normal, some of them may not even consider themselves as unemployed but as "housewives" or "retired." This new pattern implies, however, that manpower resources are not fully utilized. These people would find it natural and in their own interest to work if they had the free choice to do so. It is thus undoubtedly a restriction of liberty and opportunity.

"Retirement" from the work force also implies lower incomes. This is the more serious when the incidence of this particular type of idleness is highest in the lowest income strata, as it is apt to be. In regard to married women the effect of the husband's unemployment may be the opposite. They may find it necessary to seek work, even if it is not very regular and well paid, and though they would normally stay home with their children. The effect of unemployment then instead implies an increase of the labor force but a less socially desirable one.

The most serious thing is that there is now a visible trend of rising unemployment. The present average level is very much higher than in the forties and early fifties. Together with this rising trend of unemployment goes a tendency for the unemployed to remain out of work for a longer time. A larger proportion of the young never find employment and more old workers are unemployed or cease to seek work. Both the behavior of the unemployment figures during the recent "boomlet" and a study of the causal mechanism behind these trends make it probable that they will continue, unless radical policy measures as discussed below are applied.

To the overtly unemployed we must add the "unemployables" and the even more numerous "underemployed," *i.e.,* those workers who are left in a situation where their productivity and their wages are abnormally low. These include all those who are poor without being unemployed in the technical sense of the term. We shall touch upon this wider problem in the next chapter where we deal with the social impact of relative economic stagnation and high unemployment and, in particular, the resulting stiffening of the class structure in America by the creation of an "under-class" of more permanently unemployed, unemployables, and underemployed. In this chapter we will stick to the economic problem raised by unemployment in the more limited sense of the term.

Technological Changes

Among the causes commonly referred to in explanation of the high and rising level of unemployment in the United States are recent rapid technological changes, among them labor-saving methods of production in farming, which during the fifties have decreased the agricultural workers as part of the total civilian labor force from 12.6 to 8.5 per cent, and automation, particularly in manufacturing industry but also in wholesale and retail distribution. So far as material goods are concerned a bigger output can be produced and distributed with an ever smaller work force. Some of the major manufacturing industries in America are actually decreasing their labor demand even while raising their output of products. Practically all enterprises are curtailing their demand for particular types of labor. The increased use of electronic computing machines will also release white collar workers and those on the lower managerial level.

Generally speaking, the most important effect of technological changes on employment is that they mean a redirection of the demand for labor. Unskilled labor is less and less in demand. Even certain skills which earlier assured a relatively stable and well paid employment and a corresponding social status are becoming obsolete. This explains why the statistics on unemployment among experienced workers do not show a substantially lower growth rate than total unemployment. Workers in agriculture have to look forward to a particularly rapid decline in productive work opportunities.

Generally, labor demand is increasingly directed towards educated and trained people, particularly highly educated and trained ones working in the cities. This effect is also achieved by formalization of procedures when employing new workers. Particularly in big enterprises the educational record, questionnaires, test scores, and favorable impressions at interviews count far more than occupational skills in the ordinary and accustomed sense of the word. Thus the incidence of unemployment tends to be highest among those who for social and economic reasons and because of the location of their homes have less education and training, or, like family farmers, are stuck in an industry that increasingly needs less labor.

A structural discrepancy between labor demand and labor supply is thus created. This is illustrated by the fact that there is much overtime work at the same time as much unemployment. The overtime work is concentrated among the educated and trained, the unemployment among the less educated and trained or those whose skills are no longer needed.

Whether, besides its obvious consequences for the new direction of labor demand, the technological development can be put forward as an explanation for a general rise in unemployment—as is usually assumed—will be considered further later in this chapter.

Demographic Changes

Under conditions of a low rate of economic expansion and high unemployment the demographic changes under way tend to combine with the effects of the technological changes to release labor. There is and will continue to be a rapid increase in the labor force. By 1970 there may be $12\frac{1}{2}$ million more people at work or looking for work than there were in 1960. In comparison, the gain in the fifties was $8\frac{1}{2}$ million.

A peculiar twist to the influence of the demographic changes is due to the changing age structure of the labor force, reflecting the high birth rate during the rising employment of the war and postwar years. A total of 26 million young workers will be entering the labor force for the first time in the sixties. Nearly half of the additional people in the labor force will be under twenty-five. This contrasts sharply with any past experience for at least half a century. Less than 5 per cent of the additions to the labor force in the fifties were in that age bracket, and in the forties the figure actually declined. There will be 45 per

cent more people under twenty-five available for work in 1970 than there were in 1960. Nearly one out of four members of the labor force will then be that young.

Back in 1950, about 2 million American youths reached eighteen years of age each year; now the figure is 3 million and by 1965 it will be 4 million; it will continue on that high level through the sixties. This is a huge increase in the number of young workers seeking to find a place in a crowded labor market. In the next decade the Americans between twenty-five and forty-five will, however, barely increase in number. Those between twenty-five and thirty will actually decrease, reflecting the low birth rates of their parent generation during the Great Depression of the thirties. The oldest age group will, however, continue to increase very substantially. Those over age sixty-five will increase twice as fast in 1970 as in 1960.

It is clear that with prevailing and increasing widespread unemployment a disproportionate number of these young newcomers to the labor market will not be able to get jobs or will get jobs which they will easily lose due to low seniority and other reasons. The only means of preventing this concentration of unemployment among the young workers would be to reduce unemployment generally, and to pursue a vigorous policy to keep a much larger number of them off the labor market for education and training. Under these conditions the situation for young workers would be less hopeless if the age group above them, whom they are to follow, were shrinking or kept constant.

Meanwhile the situation for older workers, those who have passed their fifties, will deteriorate, particularly if a high and rising level of unemployment prevails.

A Closer Look at the Effects of Technological Advance on the Labor Market

The effects of technological advance on the labor market has since Ricardo's time been often discussed among economists. The debate about whether machines displace labor or open new employment opportunities at higher wages because of raised productivity has many theoretical niceties, upon which we need not enter in this context.

But it is perhaps worth-while to state as a well established historical experience that, taking the long view and disregarding short-time and isolated exceptions, technological advance in the progressive economies of the Western countries has not until now generally caused mass unemployment. In the long run it has instead been the basis for ever higher wage rates and living levels for the masses.

Mass unemployment, when it has occurred, has had its explanation in the business cycle, happening when there was a falling off of total demand. Every downturn of business has regularly seen a concentration of unemployment among the very young, the old, and the unskilled. And every upturn has meant their re-employment and, in the case of the young and the unskilled, has increased their opportunity to acquire the skills needed for employment and better employment.

In recent decades most advanced welfare states in Western Europe have learned how to control the business cycle and to stabilize high employment. It then remains a minor problem, comparatively speaking, of preventing technological advance from hurting workers: by interfering in the price formation and sometimes by providing straight subsidies as in agriculture when the outflow of workers can not be pushed and be absorbed fast enough; by stimulating through policy measures certain industries, particularly construction of homes and various community facilities; and by redirecting and increasing the possibilities for education and training of the young and providing opportunity for retraining of older workers, and so on.

But the main remedy for unemployment, independent of its causation and its character in the individual case, has been to keep total demand for products at a high and steady level and, consequently, total demand for labor constantly brisk. When this condition has been established, the readjustment of labor supply to labor demand has been accomplished without too much difficulty.

A question that must therefore be raised in relation to the American unemployment problem today is whether unemployment is really caused by technological advance in the simple way usually assumed or whether it is due to excessively low rates of growth and employment during a long period. In this context it may serve a useful purpose to touch briefly upon recent experiences of a high employment economy.

In Sweden, technological advance is also proceeding rapidly. The labor force in agriculture and forestry is decreasing almost as fast as in America. As full employment is steadily kept up, the dynamic, expanding industries—a very large part of them export industries—have from time to time experienced acute difficulties in filling their labor demand.

It is no exaggeration to state that in Sweden automation is rapidly pushed ahead by an actual or feared scarcity of human labor, and is thus looked upon by business as a means of expansion, the reliance upon which is made more necessary by a situation in the labor market which is characterized by full employment and, in the case of the expanding industries, often by labor scarcity. This is generally viewed as entirely wholesome by society at large and by the workers themselves. In America, on the contrary, automation is commonly discussed as being a main cause of unemployment.

Meanwhile Sweden is forced to spend much more to prevent unemployment than it ever did for unemployment relief in time of depression. The funds are spent productively: in paying the costs for retraining workers and for transporting and rehousing them and their families. In every economy, even the most progressive one, there are individual industries, localities, and whole regions that are regressing and where workers may be trapped if they are not helped to move.

This selective policy to prevent unemployment can raise not only employment but even more total output since it implies bringing workers to the industries where productivity is high. But a precondition for its successful pursuit is that a full employment policy is adhered to and a general scarcity of labor maintained. In such a situation the pure welfare aspect of the unemployment policy gradually fades away. This policy is an investment in higher productivity. The state is seen to be rendering a service to expanding businesses as well as to the workers threatened by unemployment. For this the business community is grateful.

From this angle it is tempting for an economist to view the American labor market problem as primarily one of low demand. What is needed would in the first instance be an economic policy that spurs total demand and thus employment. Automation would then change character and become a necessity for the dynamic enterprises in order to make it possible for them to expand under conditions of labor scarcity, instead of being a commonly recognized cause of unemployment. The government could then change its unemployment policy from relief to selective and highly productive aid to increased mobility in the labor market.

The Need for More Than Expansion

Undoubtedly there is much in this view. *The first policy inference that should be drawn from the present situation in the labor market of the United States is undoubtedly that business should be given a spurt to expand rapidly.* Otherwise every other policy measure is hopeless. And the Kennedy administration has wholeheartedly accepted that policy.

There are, however, a number of qualifications to the view that America only needs business expansion in order to cure unemployment. The Swedish policies to increase labor mobility cannot easily and rapidly be copied in the United States.

For one thing, the present situation in Sweden is characterized by the legacy of high employment, not only for a short time but during more than two decades, and of much lower unemployment even in the thirties than the United States. During this long period there have been constantly at work in Sweden all the market forces that tend to preserve the balance between demand and supply in the labor market and also in its several sectors.

On the one hand, labor has been released from many industries, in some of which, as in America, production has been rapidly increasing, without causing unemployment. This is possible since a full employment policy means that there are other occupations where labor demand has been increasing to a corresponding extent. On the other hand, the full employment situation has spurred and facilitated the individual worker's acquirement of the higher skills and the training that better fits the rapidly changing direction of the labor demand.

Fewer and in recent decades almost no workers have

been pushed down in the poverty and hopelessness of unemployment. They have thus been able to retain the spirit of enterprise, the readiness to adjustment, and the ambition for professional advance. Through their trade unions and their political participation they have actively pressed the government to provide the educational and training facilities that will fit the labor supply to the labor demand and not confine them to pockets of unemployment. This psychological and political factor should not be forgotten. There has been no "under-class" of hopeless people, conditioned to living apart from the rest of the nation.

American unemployment is instead increasingly a structural one. *Each year, indeed each month, that a high level of unemployment is tolerated makes full employment more difficult to attain as a policy goal.*

This structural character of unemployment in America means, first, that already at the present low rate of economic growth and the high and rising level of unemployment there is a scarcity of highly educated and skilled labor which shows up in the high figures for overtime by employees belonging to that elite. A rising trend of business activity would very soon be bottlenecked by a lack of this type of worker, long before the hard core of unemployed of an inferior quality had become employed. Expansion can simply not proceed very far before it meets this physical limitation, which must also have inflationary effects since their wages must tend to rise. A balanced employment situation cannot be achieved simply by business expansion.

The Superficiality of Conventional Economic Analysis

This fact that unemployment in America is structural and coexists with overfull employment in important sectors of the labor market is, of course, no discovery by the present author but is known and recognized by everybody. Curiously enough, however, much of the discussion of America's economic problems proceeds under the contrary assumption, that employment and unemployment can be dealt with as homogeneous quantities.

There is a theory which has become conventional in the whole world but which is superficial and erroneous when applied to America's present situation. It goes back to Knut Wicksell and to his various Swedish successors in the last half century, it was elaborated and improved by Maynard Keynes, and then further elaborated, improved, and complicated by hundreds and thousands of economists all over the world and not least in the United States.

Its essence is, however, simple. Aggregate demand for goods and services is counterpoised against aggregate supply, and it is not assumed as in earlier theory that they necessarily agree. Again income is divided into consumption and savings, while production is split into investment and production of consumer goods and services. Savings and investment, when counterpoised, are not assumed to be identical, except, of course, after the fact. A dissimilarity between impulses to savings and investments creates a discrepancy between aggregate demand and supply of goods and services, and this determines whether the economy is in a process of expansion or contraction.

When this theoretical model has been applied to the analysis of the economic situation and prospects of the United States, it is generally refined by breaking up all the main terms—income, production, savings, and investment—into a number of subordinate items, the relation between which is intensively studied in order to predict the short-term movement of the economy. Employment and unemployment, however, are usually left unanalyzed in that analysis, the implicit assumption being that an expansion of production will mean an increase of employment and a decrease of unemployment. Indeed, the rise of aggregate demand is assumed to be followed rather directly by a rise in demand for labor and, consequently, in employment.

This simple way of reasoning is permissible in the analysis of short-term deviations from a high level of employment. It represents, for instance, an adequate approach to the economic problems of Sweden which has a full employment economy and has had it for a long time, during which both the play of market forces and vigorous government policies have prevented structural unemployment. It is not applicable, however, to the American situation where unemployment has become structural. In an analysis of the American economy, these different types of labor demand and different categories of unemployment and their changes require the same high degree of attention that is given, for instance, to different sorts of private investment—fixed investment in the several industries, divided into new construction and producers' durable equipment, changes in inventories, home construction, and investment in consumers' durable goods, and so forth—and in the changes in the capital and money market.

Without this refinement, the analysis loses sight of a main element in the American situation, namely the structural character of unemployment which has its root in a discrepancy that has been allowed to develop between the type of labor supplied and demanded. It is, indeed, surprising to see how much of the present discussion about American relative stagnation and high unemployment is couched in terms of this new orthodoxy. It is related to the tendency to nearsightedness of American economists, politicians, and the whole articulate public upon which we shall comment in Chapter 6.

The Need for Education, Training and Retraining

The present situation of large-scale structural unemployment in the United States is caused by the absence of jobs that can easily be done by workers who are released through technological development, and by the lag in adjustment of the quality of a large portion of the young and older workers to changed labor demand.

From the policy point of view, there are two ways of overcoming the present discrepancy in America between the direction of labor demand when it is permitted to expand and the present quality of the unutilized labor supply. One way is to expand production in fields where the result will be a demand for labor of the quality that exists or can easily be acquired. The other way is to change the quality of the labor supply by education and training. As we shall see, the two types of policy-induced changes are closely interrelated.

We shall first discuss the second way of overcoming the discrepancy between the quality of labor demanded and supplied. As the technological development and the formalized procedures in employing workers continuously increase the demand for educated and highly trained workers and decrease it for the less well educated and trained, there is need for greatly increased facilities for education and training. When, moreover, we have in mind the demographic changes under way, it becomes clear that these facilities must in the first hand be placed at the disposal of young people. With the particularly rapid growth of people in the younger age groups, educational and training facilities must be expanded much more rapidly than required proportionally to the population increase.

The efforts must, moreover, particularly be directed toward the young people in those regions and those economic and social strata which now receive inadequate education and training. The fact that people in those regions and strata must have tended to become apathetic and demoralized as a result of prolonged unemployment and underemployment makes the task more difficult.

Another factor that makes a quick solution difficult or unattainable is that these facilities, particularly teachers and school buildings, must themselves be produced, which takes time even were the money available.

Besides general schooling, America needs very much greater efforts in the field of vocational training. Training for work has in America never been made a regular part of the educational system. It also needs a new philosophy. Such training, like education generally, should not be left to lead to dead ends but should help to make it possible for young people to move horizontally to other occupations and upwards to higher responsibilities as future opportunities occur.

What Negro youth in the cotton districts need is not perfection in growing cotton—and screening the windows in the shacks and tending to a garden—but a training that will help them to get out of the cotton districts and to compete for jobs in the expanding sectors of the American economy; the same is true of all farm boys and of youth in all regressive industries and localities. Vocational training should, more generally, not be focused upon acquiring skills in technologies which are on the way to being outmoded. The young need to be educated to move into and within a greater America. This is necessary in order that training shall not be wasted or even block the way to good jobs.

At the same time there is an urgent need also for the retraining of older workers in order to prevent the emergence of a group of second-class citizens who are permanently unemployed or only casually employed. We should be aware, however, that *only in an expanding economy is there a real chance of successfully rehabilitating laid-off workers or workers in the danger zone.* Sweden's highly productive employment policy has had full employment and brisk labor demand as a precondition. With widespread unemployment and little general expansion, the retrained will have difficulties in finding jobs and will easily be pushed back to their previous status. The efforts will then have been in vain and productive resources will have been wasted.

Vocational training of all types must be recognized as a duty of the government. It is true that industry, and this means predominantly big industry, is increasingly offering on-the-job education and training for its employees. Within the field of its immediate interests large industry in America is definitely a progressive force. It is now calculated that it spends almost a third of what the government—federal, state, and county—spends on formal education up to the college level. Included are formal programs and informal training which may take place during business hours or after work, in plants, offices, and classrooms with instruction given by supervisors, other staff members, or outside experts and teachers.

This is a highly commendable activity, and industry should be praised for its foresight in regard to vocational training, unsurpassed in any other Western country. Without this great effort of industry itself, the whole employment situation in the United States would look even blacker than it does. But its limitations should not be concealed. The education and training is provided mostly for those who are already employed. And for the most part it is given to those who already have a substantially high level of both education and training. It is basically a supplement and an addition to other education and training, which must be given by public institutions. It is the government in America, not private business, which has fallen behind.

The Need for Increasing Labor Demand Generally and in Special Sectors

We have stressed that the first and obvious step in a policy to eliminate the waste of large-scale unemployment must be to give the economy as much of a spurt to expansion as it safely can take with the relative scarcity of educated, trained labor. Such a spurt to expansion, if administered without forceful measures to raise the quality of the labor supply, will soon reach a ceiling which even inflation could not break. It will leave a hard core of unemployment which will be instantly increased when the boom has to be broken because of this ceiling, if for no other reason. On the other hand, without this expansion, the education and training of young people and, more particularly, the retraining of older workers will not succeed in getting more workers employed.

In addition to this policy of general economic expansion there is need for efforts to increase labor demand in special sectors of the economy. To a large extent such efforts go well with the need for raising the quality of the labor force discussed in the previous section. Thus increasing the facilities for education and training implies the necessity of providing and employing more teachers and teachers of these teachers. The same is true in the field of health and in the social services. The care, protection, and improvement of health, culture, and happiness of human beings, particularly in the lower strata, is generally less well provided for in America than in the most advanced welfare states in Western Europe.

Though technological development will also increase the productivity of the labor force engaged in service occupations, there are such huge unsatisfied needs in this sector that an expansion of its labor demand should be a main policy goal.

Meanwhile we will have to look forward to a continuation of the trend of decreasing demand for labor in manufacturing industry and in agriculture. This holds true, though to a lesser degree, even if we should follow the policy of translating into effective demand the unmet needs of the large part of the population that is not affluent; this redistributional problem will be discussed below in Chapters 3 and 4.

As a broad perspective of the future this development seems anything but discouraging. Modern society should need less and less manual labor to produce the material goods that we need. More and more of our labor force can then be engaged in educating our youth and servicing our old people, preventing and curing illnesses, advancing sciences, and intensifying and spreading culture among the whole people. But the immediate result of the decreasing demand for labor in manufacturing industry and agriculture is to release labor which cannot be retrained for the service occupations, even if by a vigorous public policy their labor demand should be made to increase rapidly. The result is also to decrease demand for those young workers who now enter the labor market without the education and training to make them fit for any tasks other than manual work.

In this situation it can almost be looked upon as a fortunate thing that America is in such dire need of rebuilding its cities, clearing its huge slums, constructing and reconstructing its obsolete and inadequate transportation system, particularly in the metropolitan districts.

All This Implies the Need for Vigorous Public Policies

Neither the increase of educational and training facilities nor the creation of increased labor demand in special sectors of the economy will come about automatically as a result of the play of the forces in the market. To create these new conditions in the labor market requires the planning and execution of public policies. So does even the primary expansion of the economy.

There is an urgent need to plan and decide upon policy action along these lines. The protracted large-scale unemployment tends itself to maintain and increase the discrepancy between the type of labor demanded and supplied that makes unemployment in America structural in character. Under conditions of a slow rate of economic growth, both technological development and demographic changes accentuate this unfortunate trend. The longer an unemployment economy is permitted to prevail, the more difficult it will be to create a rapidly and steadily expanding economy that gives full employment. Under no circumstances can the policies have instantaneous results.

These conclusions are in no way original but correspond to what labor market and educational experts are all aware of and state in one report after another, even though economists continue to reason in an unrealistic Keynesian way. They also correspond to what President Kennedy has underlined in one pronouncement after another.

That they agree with traditional American ideals of liberty and equality of opportunity is obvious. As a matter of fact the unemployment situation that is fastening itself upon the nation, and the creation of an American sub-stratum of people that have not the education and training necessary to integrate themselves in progressive American modes of life and work, challenge the very tenets of American society.

The danger is that the President will succeed in getting his policy recommendations accepted only so far as the need to start a business boom is concerned, but that he will not ask enough and, in any case, not get Congress to accept more than a very minor part of either the educational and training reforms or the work creating public undertakings that are needed in order to make it possible for an economic expansion to proceed to, and remain at, a full employment level.

America may thus have a rapid increase of its economic growth rate—for a brief time. But it will not have assured the steady growth which is what we mean by a balanced economy. And it will not have brought down unemployment more permanently and will not even have stopped the long-term trend of rising unemployment.

These opinions are contrary to two commonly held views. The one is that the United States is caught on the horn of plenty, an unavoidable dilemma of abundance, that a rapid increase of production is unnecessary and has no basis in unfilled needs, and that the goal of full employment is no longer compatible with technological advances of the character and magnitude we have seen. This view is wrong insofar as it assumes that there are no unfilled needs in America, as will be shown in the next chapter. It is furthermore a basically defeatist view. It is static and not geared to a rational approach of public responsibility and policy.

The second view is dynamic enough and policy directed, but it is superficial and false. It assumes that the level of employment is simply and directly a function of relative economic activity and means that the only thing we need is to start a business boom. But without vigorous efforts to raise the quality of labor to fit the expanding de-

mands for labor and to create more demand for manual
work in construction of various types, a boom is just a
boom and will be followed by a depression. And not even
during the boom will there be full employment.

A Note on the Proposals for a Shorter Work Week

Let me add to this the reflection that the proposals to
"share unemployment" among the workers by shortening
the work week still further do not point in a desirable direction.

The work week has in this country decreased from sixty
to forty hours in the present century, which is one of the
great gains the American people has reaped from economic progress. But neither in America, nor for that matter in any other country, has the level of culture reached
a point where more than a minority is able to make decent
use of more time between work and sleep—and that highly
educated minority is usually working much longer hours.
I believe there is support for this Puritanical attitude in recent social research.

But quite aside from the question of the desirability of
a shorter working week *per se*—which can be disputed as
it is founded on a value premise that all might not accept
—there is little reason to believe that such a change would
decrease unemployment in America, which now is largely
of a structural character. When realized for the workers who have strong union protection, of whom many are
skilled and in any case have an education and training fit
for the labor demand, it will, without increasing demand
for the bulk of the unemployed, merely tend to lower the
ceiling still further at which a boom has to be curbed be-

cause of the scarcity of such labor that is really demanded. Inflationary pressure will only spell out and accentuate the necessity of stopping expansion long before unemployment has substantially decreased. As the workers belonging to the effective trade unions where the shorter working week becomes enforced are hardly prepared to take a decrease in their earnings, the drift toward inflation will come earlier in the process with a shortened work week.*

* In Sweden, the country which I am using for comparison in this book, the normal work week is still 45 hours, though there are pressures to lower it to 40 hours. Sweden, however, has a law providing three weeks paid vacation which will now be increased by another week. If vacations cannot be spread out over the year but force employers to stop production, with the consequent underutilization of capital, vacations of this length increase costs. But in an economy with stabilized full employment and little structural unemployment, there is no ceiling lowered.

CHAPTER 3

◄╫──────────────────────────────────────╫►

Unemployment and Poverty

The Emergence of an "Under-Class"

THE facts about unemployment and its immediate causes
are well known in America due to its excellent statistical
reporting. President Kennedy has with an increasing sense
of urgency pointed to the high and rising level of unemployment as a major economic problem, even as "the major domestic challenge in the sixties." Scholarly and popular studies and newspapers follow the development of
unemployment from month to month with an eagerness
that contributes to the whole nation's awareness of this
misuse of its productive resources.

Less often observed and commented upon is the tendency of the changes under way to trap an "under-class" *
of unemployed and, gradually, unemployable and underemployed persons and families at the bottom of a society,
while for the majority of people above that layer the increasingly democratic structure of the educational system
creates ever more real liberty and equality of opportunity,
at least over the course of two generations.

---

* The word "under-class" does not seem to be used in English.
In America where, as opinion polls over several decades show, the
great majority reckon themselves as "middle class," this is particularly understandable on ideological grounds. Nevertheless, the
term will be used in this book as the only one adequate to the social reality discussed.

The American self-image was, and is, that of a free and open society where anyone who is of a sound body and soul and has the drive can find work, at least when business is on the upturn, and where he can climb to the highest and most rewarding positions. It was this image, and the considerable degree of reality that actually corresponded to it, that induced millions of poor people in Europe to seek their opportunity in America right up to the First World War.

Reality never agreed entirely with that image. And over the last few generations a process has been under way that, while it opened more opportunities to more people, also closed ever more opportunities to some. Now in the end it threatens to split off a true "under-class" that is not really an integrated part of the nation but a useless and miserable substratum.

To start at the heights, the "self-made man" with great wealth and a supreme command over men and productive resources has been disappearing in America ever since the time when college education became so common that a man without a degree could hardly advance in business. Business itself has tended to become increasingly large-scale and highly organized. This process was well under way over half a century ago. One element in the American image—symbolized by the boy who sold newspapers or shined shoes but became an industrial, commercial, or financial tycoon, or by the man who fought his way from the log cabin to the White House—has had to be written off.

A basic cause for this process was a gradual democratization of higher education. In this America had, and still has, the lead in the Western world. The journey to the top could, and still can on the basis of schooling, be done in two generations even if not in one man's lifetime.

Moreover, even if the highest economic and social positions were closed to those who started from the bottom, it was still possible to advance and advance far in many occupations, and in practically every field there was an expansion of opportunity for a long time. In addition, there was at least plenty of unskilled work to be done and, when business was good, there was always demand for it. After the end of the Great Depression this was still so in the war years and in the early postwar boom.

We have to remind ourselves, however, that to a considerable extent this American image was always something of a myth. Even leaving out the highest social and economic positions that have now been closed up to those starting without higher education, the opportunity to rise in society, or even to maintain a decent and respectable level of living and to participate in the nation's general culture and the solution of its problems, was not always that open in the old days. Great masses of people had no possibility of sharing in the American image of liberty and opportunity of rising economically and socially. This applied to the cotton farming Negro tenants in the South, the white hillbillies not far south of Washington, D. C., and similar groups of poor whites elsewhere in the country, the migrant workers on the big California farms, and to the workers in the sweatshops in the cities. Moreover, partly overlapping with the last category, there were the new immigrants in the city slums, handicapped in many ways, who often suffered miserable hardships before they came into their own.

Finally, in the periodic slowdowns in business activity a large number even of well integrated workers found themselves unemployed and without an income. The series of such reverses culminated in the Great Depression when up to 20 per cent or more of the labor force was unemployed.

Abject destitution for millions of people is thus nothing new in America. The trend has definitely been to decrease the number suffering from it or even running a major risk of it. Major causes of this have been the rising productivity of the American economy and also the facts that educational facilities have been vastly improved and that good schools and college education have been placed at the disposal of an ever increasing portion of the people, earlier and more generously than in any other Western country.

The New Threat

Nevertheless, there is something threatening in the very recent changes and in the trend for the foreseeable future. The displacement of unskilled and even of much skilled labor has a definiteness that must compel us to stop and think. To take advantage of the expansion of demand for highly educated and trained labor, which is occurring and would do so even more rapidly if the growth rate of the economy were higher, would require such education and training of the displaced that he simply cannot think of jumping the gap, no matter how alert and enterprising he is. He needs to be helped to do it by society or he will not be able to do it at all.

What is happening is similar to the disappearance more than half a century ago of the "self-made man" from the highest positions as a result of the widening of college education and training for leadership in business as it increasingly became large-scale, organized, and stratified. This process has continued steadily downwards, first to middle positions and then to ever lower strata of employees in industry and commerce, until it is now beginning to make unskilled and many skilled workers redundant.

This is a new threat. For when the process has proceeded that far, without a parallel change for educating and training the *whole* labor force to correspond to the new demands, there is no longer any vast space left beneath for economic advance and social mobility as when the self-made man at the top disappeared. Those not needed are true "outcasts." They simply become unemployed, and indeed largely unemployable, or underemployed. It is almost as difficult for them to get and hold a good job as it long ago became to start as a shoe-shine boy and end as the president of a big corporation.

This emergence of an American "under-class" of unemployed and largely unemployable and underemployed occurs at a time when almost the last batches of immigrants from Southern and Eastern Europe and their descendants have finally become integrated in the American nation. It happens when those educated and trained to fit the new direction of labor demand are experiencing a brisk demand for their work, and when the general levels of living of the majority of well employed Americans—and thereby the general conception spread by the mass-communication industry of what the American way of life is like—have risen high above what a few generations ago were considered comfortable standards. In society at large there is more equality of opportunity today than there ever was. But for the bottom layer there is less or none.

The disappearance of the self-made man was a slight change in society compared to that now under way, closing all good jobs and soon almost all jobs worth having in affluent America to those who have happened to be born in regions, localities, or economic and social strata where education and training for life and work in this new America are not provided as a normal thing. For the larger part of America there is social and economic mobility through the educational system. Beneath that level a line is drawn to an "under-class." That class line becomes demarcated almost as a caste line, since the children in this class tend to become as poorly endowed as their parents.

In a situation of high and rising unemployment even the trade unions often, unwillingly, become instrumental in hardening the line which excludes that substratum of workers from opportunities of getting jobs. The process of automation is particularly extensive in sectors of the American economy in which there are effective trade unions. These unions are thus forced to press for job security for their own members even when this creates incentives for the employers not to engage new workers. In a situation of high unemployment the unions also often feel their bargaining strength weakened and find it difficult to dissipate too much of it by taking a consistent and strong stand for what is the main interest from all the workers' point of view, full employment.

They are thus in danger of being reduced to protective organizations for a number of separate groups of job holders. Even if the unions are taken all together, they only represent a minority, perhaps one quarter, of all workers. And as long as their members have jobs they belong to the middle class in the nation. In this connection, we should not forget that labor protectionism has old traditions in the American trade union movement, particularly in the A.F. of L. craft unions. To an observer it seems almost a miracle that big units of the movement, particularly the industrial unions in the C.I.O. wing, have found it possible to take such broadminded and progressive positions on national economic issues as they actually have.

The fact that the substratum is not very articulate in America and is, therefore, not much noticed by the ordinary, well educated Americans who are busily and happily enjoying both their work and their leisure, does not detract from the gravity of this development. On the contrary, it is fatal for democracy, and not only demoralizing for the individual members of this under-class, that they are so mute and without initiative and that they are not becoming organized to fight for their interests. For its own health and even preservation an effective, full-fledged democracy needs movements of protest on the part of the underprivileged.

The Curse of Unemployment

During the Great Depression, studies in America and many other Western countries showed that a very large percentage of those unemployed were on the way to becoming "unemployables." Although almost all of these potential unemployables rapidly disappeared when the demand for labor revived during and after the war, we cannot in the present state of affairs in America have confidence that the same would now happen, even if we could suddenly and substantially lift the curve of economic growth.

This time, increased labor demand will to a higher extent be directed toward skilled and educated workers, leaving a large part of the others out. It is discouraging but probably realistic when the Kennedy administration has redefined tolerable unemployment to be as high as 4 per cent, apparently not reckoning part-time unemployment and underemployment at low productivity levels.

There is even a probability that the level of unemployment may be higher still when a boom has to be broken, ultimately, because of the scarcity of educated and trained workers, if for no other reason. This will leave a hard core of unemployment that is uncomfortably high.

Unemployment is a damaging way of life. It is particularly damaging for the young in the nation, and even more particularly when their educational and cultural level is low. Crime, prostitution, and all sorts of shady ways of passing time will thrive as they did in the slums during the depression years in the thirties and as they increasingly begin to do today.

The well meaning proposals, put forward by progressive writers, for paying greatly increased unemployment benefits or sometimes even full wages without time limit to those who have been thrown out of work through no fault of their own, have, of course, little chance of being accepted by Congress. But apart from their lack of political realism, such proposals underestimate how unhealthy and destructive it is for anybody and particularly for young people without much share in the national culture to go idle and live more permanently on doles—this tenet of old-fashioned Puritanism, I believe, is also fully borne out by recent social research. Work is not only, and not even mainly, a "disutility" as conceived by the classical economist. It is, if not always a pleasure, the basis for self-respect and a dignified life. There is no real cure for unemployment except employment, which does not mean, of course, that it is not important to make it possible for people to live when they have become unemployed.

A Vicious Circle

The essential question when probing into the social impact of the formation of this under-class is the character of the selective process which determines whether a man comes above or beneath the dividing line. The selection operates on the criterion of education and training. When old people have failed, and young people are now failing, to get an education up to levels which correspond to national standards and the direction of the demand for labor, the explanation is usually that they have been living in an environment of poverty and squalor.

It has become customary to describe the situation in underdeveloped countries as one of a vicious circle where "poverty perpetuates itself." But the same vicious circle operates in an underprivileged class in the richest country.* To begin with, unemployment means loss of income. Particularly for those who become permanently unemployed and for those whose employment is casual and in fields not covered by unemployment compensation, the lost income is total or very substantial.

They will become disheartened and apathetic. As parents they will not be able to pay toward such support of the education of their children that would be needed. Instead, they will have an incentive to take them out of school early if any employment, even at low wages and promising no secure future, offers itself. The home environment of the unemployed and poor will generally be less conducive for children and youth to become educated and trained for good jobs.

The unemployed will be forced to live in the slums or, more probably, they will always have lived in the slums. Whatever the regulations are, the schools will be bad in the slums as they will be in the districts where the backwoods farmer lives. And the whole way of life in the crowded slum quarters in the cities or the rural slum districts will be destructive for the will and ability to advance in life.

A remarkable tendency in America has been that parallel and prior to the rise in unemployment the efforts of slum clearance in the cities have mainly benefited the middle third of the nation who could afford to pay the rents in the new houses which only to a smaller extent have really been "low-cost housing." Those made homeless have been pressed into other already crowded slum districts or into districts which in this process of change became slum districts.

This perverted tendency in American housing policy

* For an early statement of the theory of circular causation resulting in a cumulative process and of its application to an underprivileged category of people in a rich country, see *An American Dilemma* (New York, Harper, 1944), Chapter 3, Section 7, "The Theory of the Vicious Circle," pp. 78 ff., and Appendix 3, "A Methodological Note on the Principle of Cumulation," pp. 1035 ff.

has its parallel in almost all other social policies. Various social security schemes as well as to an extent the minimum wage regulations happen to stop just above the very neediest groups of people. The voluntary health insurance schemes are much too expensive for the poorest who show the highest incidence of illness and ill health, both mental and bodily. In the same way agricultural policy has mainly aided the big and progressive farmers and has done little if anything for small farmers, small tenants, and agricultural workers. It is true that most of them should be moved out of agriculture, but little is done to speed the process, to prepare them not to end up unemployed or underemployed in the slums.

There is a political factor in this vicious circle of circular causation leading to a cumulative process. The poor in America are unorganized and largely mute. They exert no pressure corresponding to their numbers and to the severity of their plight. They are the least revolutionary proletariat in the world. As the studies of registration and election participation show, they are largely responsible for the comparatively low percentage of voters in America, and this not only in the South where the Negroes are still largely kept from voting even if they wanted to, but in the rest of the country, as well.

As they represent the big unutilized reserve of potential voters, the platforms of both Democrats and Republicans worked out before every election will regularly seem to imply a radical departure from policies pursued up till then—though most often couched in general and noncommittal terms. When the elections are over, however, and many of the poor are seen to have still stayed away from the polls, actual policies return to the routine of not doing much for them.

The Minority Groups

Much of the rising unemployment falls upon minority groups and implies a serious setback in the process of national integration. The largest and still most handicapped minority group in America is that of the Negroes.

From about the beginning of the last war there has been a definite trend toward improved race relations in America, a development which is the more remarkable as for sixty years up till that time there had been no great change in the status of the Negroes in America. A very important cause among others of this encouraging trend was undoubtedly the rising level of labor demand from the beginning of the war and after the Great Depression. An increasing number of Negroes were allowed to acquire skills, join trade unions, and get seniority and job protection in new fields that were opening themselves for Negroes.

But the Negroes are still the "last hired and the first fired." Negro unemployment is presently about three times as high as the average rate, which means that close to a fifth of the Negro workers are unemployed. Apart from a tiny upper and middle class of professionals and business people, mostly thriving behind the remaining walls of prejudice, and now a considerably increased group of skilled and union protected workers, the majority of Negroes are much poorer and have had less education and training than the average white Americans. They are consequently more vulnerable in the present situation where labor demand is, and must be, turning towards those who have been educated and trained.

They are also directly discriminated against, legally and illegally, when seeking a home. Negro slums are getting the more overcrowded and dilapidated for this reason. In the South the whole educational system still mainly segregates them in inferior schools. All other acts of prejudice and discrimination tend to press the Negroes down economically and socially. The trend in these other respects has, as I said, been toward improvement from the beginning of the Second World War. But the reforms are slow to work themselves out in terms of substantial changes in the Negroes' living conditions.

High and rising unemployment among Negroes is, on the one hand, an aggravating cause, in many ways hampering the rise in status of the American Negroes. On the other hand, these inferior living conditions, including inadequate education and training, tend to make it more difficult for Negroes to get and hold the good jobs.

The greatest danger threatening the gratifying upward trend in race relations in America stems from this vicious circle, operating in a situation of generally high and rising unemployment, when inferior living conditions cause a proportionally much heavier incidence of unemployment among Negroes, while the spread of unemployment in its turn causes a deterioration of living conditions.*

But to the large number of Negro workers—more than 10 per cent of the labor force—who more than others are hit by unemployment when it is high and rising, and to the Puerto Ricans, the Mexicans, and other minority groups affected in the same way, must be added poor white people everywhere in America who will be pressed down, and by the vicious circle held down, in this substratum which is excluded from the prosperity of the nation at large and the progress of the American way of life.

* Some further observations on the problems of the American Negroes in present day America are contained in the Appendix.

Poverty

The Bureau of the Census, several of the departments in Washington and of the state administrations, university institutions, and other research outfits have in recent years done a commendable job of laying bare the facts of American poverty and of the causal relations behind this poverty.

They give a consistent and clear picture of the situation, with not more divergence between the different computations than is inherent in a process of statistical observations and definitions. The summary condensation below of the results of these various studies is derived from *Poverty and Deprivation in the U.S.*, published by the Conference on Economic Progress (Washington, 1962), which has taken them all into consideration and properly accounted for the methods used to arrive at the figures.

If poverty is defined as having to live on an annual income under $4,000 for multiple-person families and $2,000 for unattached individuals, 38 million Americans, or more than one fifth of the nation, were poor in 1960. In deprivation, above poverty but short of the requirements for what in America is now considered a modestly comfortable level of living—from $4,000 to $6,000 for families and from $2,000 to $3,000 for unattached individuals—were more than 39 million people, or again more than one fifth of the nation. Utter destitution, estimated to be the situation of people with less than half of the income representing the poverty line, was the destiny of more than 12½ million Americans, or nearly 7 per cent of the population in the United States.

The proportion of people in these different categories of deprivation, poverty, and destitution has been decreasing since the depression years, first rapidly and then slowly. The slowdown has become particularly marked during the last decade. The proportion of the destitute with incomes under half the level taken to be the poverty line has actually increased a little. The income distribution in the whole nation did follow a tendency towards gradual equalization until the last decade when the relative economic stagnation reflected itself in a new tendency to increasing economic inequality in the nation.

Poverty is greater in the South. It is more than twice as common among the nonwhite population all over the country. More than three times as many nonwhites as whites have less than half of the income taken to demarcate the poverty line.

Poverty is also greater in agriculture. It there afflicts the small farmers, the small tenants, and the hired workers who make up the majority of rural people. About two thirds of the latter group earned less than $1,000 a year.

Much more frequently poverty hits families whose head is female, whether they have lost a husband and father or never had one. People over sixty-five years of age are particularly poor in America. Of those aged sixty-five and having a family, close to two thirds lived in poverty and nearly one third were destitute, according to the definitions given above. Indeed, one tenth of the families had to live on less than $1,000 a year which means utter destitution. The lonely elderly persons were even worse off. Four fifths lived in poverty and nearly half were destitute. The median income of families with heads aged sixty-five and over was under $3,000 and of unattached individuals only a little over $1,000. This age group is now increasing almost twice as fast as ten years ago.

Low income is closely related to the amount of schooling people have had. Among families whose heads had less than eight years of elementary education almost two thirds lived in poverty with incomes under $4,000. More than one third had under $2,000. Among the unattached individuals the incidence of poverty was even heavier.

The less well educated families and unattached individuals accounted for far more than half of those living in poverty. The correlation between health deficiencies and low incomes is similar.

More than 40 per cent of the families whose heads were unemployed lived in poverty. They constituted a fourth of the total population living in poverty. The other three fourths had occupations for which we have invented the new term "underemployed" when analyzing the development problems in underdeveloped countries in order to characterize people who have been stuck in localities and jobs on a low level of productivity and, consequently, of earnings.

To the underemployed in this sense belong the larger part of the agricultural population of which the progressive, and prosperous, mainly large-scale farm operators, are a minority. In the cities they have low-paid jobs, often of a casual nature.

Increased Inequality in the Midst of General Equality

It is perfectly possible for the majority of Americans to live, together with practically everybody they have primary contact with, in a situation of full and even overfull employment where there is brisk demand and competition for their labor, while they read in the newspapers that there is large and growing unemployment beneath them. That this can be so is the result of the nature of unemployment being to a large extent structural in character.

While this is happening at the bottom of American society it is perfectly possible that there is ever greater social mobility, liberty, and equality of opportunity and a generally rising economic and cultural level in majority America. More and more individuals and families may move further away from the neighborhood of the dividing line. Social welfare policies have, as I pointed out, been framed to give greater security especially for that middle group in the nation. And there might even be some successful passing of the poverty line by individuals coming from beneath it, which then gives a false assurance that America is still the free and open society of its cherished image and well established ideals.

But as less and less work is required of the type the people in the urban and rural slums can offer, they will be increasingly isolated and exposed to unemployment, to underemployment, and to plain exploitation. There is an ugly smell rising from the basement of the stately American mansion.

CHAPTER 4

Liberty and Equality

The Central Issue in the Economic Stagnation Problem

The Moral Issue

THE facts that, firstly, everything is so good for the majority of Americans and, secondly, that America has had to live for such long periods with the problems of undigested minorities of various sorts, from the former Negro slaves to the more recent immigrants from Southern and Eastern Europe, go a long way to explain the complacency among average, good, and warmhearted upper and middle class Americans about the staggering extent to which a large number of their compatriots are poor, indeed very poor, and lacking in elementary opportunities which the average American takes for granted for himself and his children and for everybody in his own milieu.

He can travel into a city and vaguely see the big and miserable slums without recognizing as a living reality that they exist and that thousands and hundreds of thousands, even millions, of families are confined to live in them. He can glance through the newspapers, and learn in an abstract way how much more has to be spent by the community in the slum districts on police, fire protection, health, emergency aid, and the like, and how, in spite of these provisions, there is much more crime and prostitution, illegal gambling and gangsterism, houses on fire, debilities and chronic illnesses, as well as epidemics and short-term sicknesses, alcoholism and mental illnesses, and so on, in the slums than in the type of well kept and clean suburb where he lives. He knows that infant mortality is higher there, as is the rate at which mothers die at childbirth.

The educated American also knows since several decades that, as a general proposition, the higher incidence of all these unfortunate things among the poor is usually not due to inborn differences in human quality but is caused by the environment. In a queer contradiction of this theoretical knowledge, he posits a sort of general moral feeling that nobody needs to be unemployed and poor unless he is a bad person.

Nevertheless, it remains something of a mystery that the majority of Americans show such lack of concern about these facts. The mystery becomes the greater when we recall the predominance in America of what I have been accustomed to referring to as "Christian neighborliness." There is, as everybody should know who is well acquainted with the country, a basic sentiment in America of generosity toward those who are less fortunate—a sympathy for, and solidarity with, the underdog. This has roots in America's singular material and spiritual history. On this score America is very different from Western Europe.

The American's purse is more open for charity than that of people in other nations. When observing that America could wait until the Great Depression and the New Deal to begin to develop a welfare policy it should not be forgotten that America had, and still has, the world's most generous and best organized private charity.* Every call for charity from abroad, to relieve the victims of earthquakes or other calamities, has always met with a much more generous response in America than in

* *Kontakt med America* (Stockholm 1941), p. 154, *An International Economy* (New York, 1956), p. 122.

other countries. America's missionary work in poor lands has been magnificent over several generations.

It is only when the problem presents itself as a question of redistributing incomes and organizing collective consumption through public measures that the majority of Americans can be seen to become hardhearted and stingy. Even on that point a very important qualification has to be made. America was early to reorganize every child's right to free elementary education, and a number of American states even wrote that right into their constitutions. Thereafter it democratized higher education far ahead of all other nations, and we have in the foregoing pages referred to the beneficial effect of this on the development of American society. However, this opportunity never became fully realized for the very poorest in the nation.

When the Second World War ended, the United States undertook a publicly organized international redistribution on a large scale—in favor of foreign countries, in the first hand those in Western Europe. The big rescue action under the Marshall Plan will be discussed in Chapter 10. In the present context the main thing to stress is that this was a charity under the management of the government and paid for by the American taxpayers. That it was chiefly motivated by generosity towards the unfortunate is not disproved by the fact that the Americans tried to persuade themselves and others that they did it out of self-interest.*

* "It does not require any comprehension or deep study of the American motives for this extraordinary aid to say from first-hand observation of the American people that, in the beginning, the main attitude was much more the positive one of sympathy and solidarity, rather than the negative one of fear of Communism. . . . It is true that the Americans tried eagerly to convince themselves at the very inauguration of the Marshall Plan that they were acting solely with their own national interest in view, but this was only a further example of the strange suspicion on the part of the American people of their own generous motives, which I once analyzed as a slightly perverted element of their Puritan tradition." *An International Economy* (New York, Harper, 1956), p. 122.

In a queer way, the American's reluctance to more concretely recognize all the poverty at home made it more possible for him to go in wholeheartedly for the idea that his government should be prepared to aid foreign countries. Indeed, the average American shared himself the general view that established itself after the war throughout the world that the United States is an immensely rich country which, without much contribution from other countries, should take upon itself meeting all needs for assistance wherever they appeared in the world. When traveling abroad or meeting foreigners at home his belief in affluence was giving support to this view.

When he later was brought to change this attitude, it was mainly because of the foreign exchange difficulties appearing some five years ago. The fact that he still gave the appearance of seeing his own country as immensely rich often led foreigners to feel that the Americans are coldhearted, which is the opposite of the truth. It became the duty of foreign friends to recall some simple truths:

> Though foreigners have been led to forget it, and sometimes Americans too, the United States also has city slums which it wants to rebuild; in many parts of the country the need is felt for more classrooms and more teachers, and it is generally recognized that the teachers are underpaid; many remote areas are pleading for modern medical facilities. And there are many courthouses and Post Office buildings, bridges, and dams that have not been erected because the budget was too tight.*

* *An International Economy,* p. 128.

Eradication of Poverty as an Economic Interest and a Necessity for Economic Progress

The moral issue has been touched upon as it is important, particularly so in the American nation which is basically moralistic and, at bottom, not very cynical. The "hard-boiled" social scientists in America, who are trying to forget that people have consciences and that this fact is of importance in the social and political processes, are wrong. More specifically they are reacting according to a common perversion of the nation's Puritanism.

Since the eradication of poverty in America has now become an economic interest and almost a political necessity if America is to get out of the rut of relative economic stagnation with high and rising unemployment and underemployment, it is easy to forecast that moves for reform will come to be supported by strong moral sentiments. There is already a rising tide of moralism in the public debate on this issue as carried on in the literature and the press and by the political and intellectual leaders of the nation. The production of the comprehensive statistics I have quoted is itself an indication of the moral upsurge. Of the same nature is the flood of books on American poverty currently being written.

However, I now leave the moral issue and turn to the economics of the matter and to the policies that would turn the trend toward rapid and steady economic growth. In Chapter 2, unemployment was first related to the discrepancy between the direction of labor demand and the quality of labor supply which gives the present unemployment its structural character. We found that, though the first condition for a reduction of unemployment must be a spurt to economic expansion, this will not take the country far towards full employment. Technological change will continue to release manual labor in agriculture and manufacturing industry, and the number of young workers entering the labor market without training for anything but manual labor will be increasing.

In order to reach full employment, public policy measures will have to be taken to raise the demand for such labor, mainly in construction work of various types. In order to enable the labor supply to meet this policy-induced increase and redirection of labor demand, large-scale training and retraining of workers will be needed. For the permanent achievement of full employment, huge reforms are needed in the field of education, including vocational training. These efforts will have to be directed primarily to the poverty-stricken sectors of the American society where unemployment and underemployment are concentrated and where the present opportunities are unsatisfactory.

These efforts have to be made and the expenditures paid for by public authority. The policy measures have to be planned for gradual realization. Under no circumstances can the goal be reached immediately. As high and rising unemployment is apt continually to worsen the preconditions for this type of policy, it is urgent that a start be made right away and on a large enough scale.

In Chapter 3 we revealed the complex web through which a low level of education and training and, generally, low quality of labor supply is interrelated with poverty and all that poverty implies. The conclusion is that to be successful a full employment policy must aim at gradually eradicating poverty.

Efforts to educate and train the young and to re-educate those grown-ups who need it must meet with greater difficulties, be much less effective and, consequently, even from a financial point of view imply more waste, the longer these people are poor, live in urban and rural slums, and are afflicted by all the other consequences of poverty. To an extent, but as we know from experience only to an extent, poverty will decrease as an effect of economic expansion and fuller employment. Direct measures of a surgical nature are needed at the same time. And they can be taken with less financial sacrifice on the part of the better-offs if the economy is progressing—indeed, so I am convinced, without any real sacrifice at all.

So far we have been discussing policies to change the supply of labor in order that it should better meet the demand for labor. However, an economic policy aimed at a reversal of the present trend of relative stagnation is even more fundamentally dependent upon an attack on poverty. The first condition for bringing down unemployment and for gradually reaching a full employment situation in America is certainly an expansion of production. Policy measures to induce an expansion of production imply an expansion of aggregate demand.

As a short-run proposition an increase of aggregate demand can be achieved by a great variety of policies. Nothing is technically simpler than to start a boom. It could be done by spreading dollar notes as fertilizer from aeroplanes. From that point of view, and as the main thing is to get the economy going at full speed, it might seem that it should not be of great importance what particular policy measures are chosen.

But as the goal must be to reach not only a rapid but also a steady growth of the economy, it becomes important to be careful in choosing the policy means. The structural character of the present unemployment which we discussed in Chapter 2 makes it important that there be public investment in education, training, and retraining of workers right from the start. Otherwise scarcity of personnel with high levels of education and training will soon set a ceiling to the rise in production and most probably cause a recession long before anything in the neighborhood of full employment is achieved. As a low quality of part of the labor supply is intertwined with poverty in a vicious circle, there are reasons to take vigorous measures, also from the very start, to reduce poverty.

All this implies public expenditures which in the first place will improve the lot of the poor in America. The reason why such a redistributional economic policy will be of a general economic interest and not only benefit the poor themselves is, of course, that their unemployment and their low productivity when they are working is the main unutilized and underutilized resource in America. The majority of Americans now living in comfortable circumstances should as a result of this policy become better and not worse off than now. To get this dynamic thought understood and widely accepted is a major task for all efforts to public enlightenment in America.

The problem of economic expansion will first be dealt with in this chapter on the assumption that adequate measures are taken to prevent internal inflation and a deterioration of the country's international exchange position. In the next chapter the analysis will be completed by a study of what this implies in regard to economic policies.

The Unmet Needs

Our account of the actual extent of poverty in America proves that the popular view of the great abundance and affluence of American society is highly exaggerated. A fifth of the American people is now officially recognized to be living in poverty. Of these a very substantial part are really destitute. And above the poverty-stricken fifth of the nation there are at least as many who do not share in any substantial way in the abundance believed to be characteristic of America. For a large minority the affluent society is nothing but a myth.

I am convinced that if my friend Kenneth Galbraith—

with his keen sense for the need of the hour and his dislike of conventional wisdom—were to rewrite his book *The Affluent Society* today, he would write a very different work, indeed a book challenging some views he himself has contributed to make conventional: that America is affluent and that increasing production is no longer a main problem. This view which is now so popular is undoubtedly responsible for much undue complacency about American economic growth and even for a widespread feeling among Americans that the limit for further expansion of the economy is near.

The fact is, of course, that there is a very large volume of crying elementary needs in America which, if they were translated into effective demands, could sustain rapid economic growth of production for a long time to come. They could do this even without the efforts of the advertising industry to induce the really affluent Americans to ever more fancy consumption patterns which stand in such blunt contradiction to the nation's inherited Puritan ideals.

There is, however, so much solid truth in the appreciation of the technological revolution under way and of the capacity of the American economy to expand production of material goods in almost every field, if a higher growth rate were permitted, that a rise in the living standards for the underprivileged becomes an almost necessary condition for long-term rapid advance. Even apart from the urgency to improve the quality of that part of the labor force that is otherwise not required or being underemployed in low-productivity occupations, and *already in order to build a more solid foundation in aggregate demand for expansion of production, large-scale redistributional reforms are urgently called for.*

Redistributional Reforms

Redistributional reforms should be looked upon as equally important as a basis for the achievement of rapid and steady expansion of the American economy and high employment as from the point of view of social justice.

The reform that implies least government intervention in the economy is, of course, a reduction of the tax burden in the lower income brackets. The prevalence in the tax system of the United States—including the states and the municipalities—of taxes on real property and of sales taxes of various sorts implies, as a recent study by the Tax Foundation has revealed, that the tax burden in the lower and middle income strata is decisively regressive. This cannot possibly be in accordance with the nation's ideals for the distribution of the tax burden. A reform is overdue and would immediately put more purchasing power in the hands of those in America who are not consuming enough.

Nor would urgently needed reforms of the social security system require much government intervention in the economy. In this field the United States is still far behind the countries that share its basic values.

The treatment of old people in America, many of whom have a hard life behind them, is remarkable. Some basic facts illustrating the terrifying extent to which old people are left in poverty and destitution were given in the last chapter. They and their families, insofar as they have any, now represent one third of all poor people in America, a proportion that, if things are left as they are, will be increasing as their portion of the total population rises. It cannot possibly be the considered opinion of the majority of Americans that so many of those who in America are often called "senior citizens" should be left in misery, squalor, and often forbidding loneliness, unattended though they are in need of care. The situation is overripe for a radical reform of the old age security system.

In Sweden all persons over sixty-seven will now, in stable currency, be guaranteed an income which, up to a fairly high level, shall amount to two thirds of what they earned in their best years. That the age limit could be placed so high is explained, first by the fact that there is a more accomplished system of social security for the sick, the invalid, and other needy groups. Moreover, in a full employment economy old people find a demand for their labor. As a matter of fact many over sixty-seven are also working. And more of them would be, if there was not an unfortunate tax rule discouraging them from having extra incomes; this tax rule will be changed in the continuous routine work on perfecting the details of the welfare state. The main problem left which is now eagerly discussed is how the economic security for the old can be supplemented by more of human care, so that old people should not be left so lonely in meeting their problems of life.

The United States is equally rich as Sweden. Most Americans believe they are much richer. They could certainly afford to be more generous to the old generation. In fact, I sincerely believe that the great majority of Americans, if they really were fully aware of the facts and saw the problem, should be eager to do it.

Likewise, it is impossible that the majority of good Americans really think that so many widows, divorced women, and unmarried mothers with their children should be left largely unaided. They also constitute one third of the poor in America.

The same must be true of the many families who are forced into poverty or destitution because the number of their children is so large. There are apparently no comprehensive statistics on the situation of families with numerous children. But from studies in other countries we know the crucial importance of this relationship. America is far behind most other rich countries in taking policy measures to prevent children from becoming a cause of poverty for their families and, at the same time, creating severe handicaps for their own advance in life.

Then we have the invalid and the sick. America can, of course, not long postpone creating a comprehensive system of pensions for invalids and of health insurance. It is possible, although difficult to imagine, that America may succeed in building up its health insurance system to a greater part on the basis of voluntary insurance schemes than have other countries more advanced in this as in other fields of social welfare policy. But such a solution will then need to be supplemented by very substantial contributions from the government in order not to leave unaided so many of those who most need health protection and medical care, and who cannot afford to pay the premiums for private insurance.

The improvement of the unemployment benefit system, particularly for the underemployed and the casually employed, belongs to the needed reforms of social security. It is not only a question of raising the level of unemployment benefits but of making them available on a national scale for all unemployed, even those having a shifting and menial job or not employed for a period long enough to qualify under present rules. The financial burden of an improvement of this form of social security—as of most others—will tend to be heaviest in the beginning, but to taper off as the economy expands and full employment is restored.

Related to social security reforms are a number of other reforms that do not require direct state intervention in the running of the economy. Thus it is urgently important that the minimum wage legislation be made comprehensive and not as now inapplicable in many of the occupations where the setting of a wage floor is particularly important, as for instance in hotels and restaurants, some retail stores, hospitals, and laundries. Even after the change in the minimum legislation two years ago, some 16 million workers are not covered.

It is obvious that it is in the public interest that the mass of poor workers in these and in other low-paid jobs become organized in regular trade unions—and protected from exploitation by union racketeers. The task of organizing the majority of American workers who are outside the trade unions is, though not very forcefully, pursued by the American trade union movement. The success of these efforts will be more assured, and the progress much more rapid, if the American economy is firmly set on the road to rapid and steady expansion.

The government itself, however, must take the responsibility of supplementing its agricultural policies in such a way that small farmers, small tenants, and farm workers are not left in poverty and destitution. In order not to make them permanent dole-takers, action will have to be taken to speed up the migration from rural slums, which again implies education, training, and retraining of the young and old workers settled there. Such policies also will have substantial results only when the economy is expanding rapidly and steadily.

Other Governmental Action

So far we have touched upon redistributive schemes that can be operated mainly on a cash basis or, in any case, without much government intervention in the economy. It should be clear, however, that in addition to those reforms there is a need for government policies that involve the government more directly in steering the economy, mostly by providing enterprise and services that properly belong to the public sector since they cannot be expected to be forthcoming from private business. This, incidentally, is not a criticism of private business. Its proper role in the national economy of a democracy is to produce, sell, and make a profit as high as possible under the conditions created by the government but not to create those conditions itself.

In Chapter 2 we have already dealt with the urgent need of much greater efforts in the field of education and training of the young, particularly in the poorer strata, and of retraining old workers now afflicted by unemployment or employed in low-productivity occupations. We have also pointed out that this is not a simple matter, as teachers have to be educated and trained first. Implied is the need for a radical and comprehensive educational plan and an unemployment policy directed to rehabilitation and reallocation of workers.

Almost the same is true in regard to health protection and medical care. The training of doctors and nurses must be considerably expanded and speeded up.

In filling these needs it will be necessary to allocate much larger resources to building schools and hospitals. In regard to the last item of badly needed increases of investment it may be useful to compare the United States with Sweden, which is now far ahead of America both in regard to hospital beds per thousand inhabitants and the yearly increase of that important index. Even if President Kennedy's extremely limited proposal of medical aid to the aged were enacted—while it does not meet the full need for hospital care for the chronically ill and does not pay for doctors and medicine—this would release a big demand that is now unsatisfied for hospital beds and also, of course, for doctors and nurses.

But there are many other public investments which are now irrationally neglected. There is, of course, no excuse for a rich country to tolerate huge slums in the big cities and lesser ones in the smaller cities, at the same time as it allows a large part of its manpower and other productive resources to go to waste. We have already pointed out that until now public efforts in the way of slum clearance have been feeble and mostly perverted in a way to favor the middle third of the nation but leave the poor in often worse slums than before. This has been the reality behind the euphemistic term "urban renewal"—which in Detroit is popularly referred to as "Negro removal."

Closely related to the slum clearance problem are all the other huge investments needed to make the American cities more effective as containers of human life and efficient work. These public investments become more urgently needed since now more than the total population increase goes to swell the number of city dwellers and, in particular, the number of the inhabitants of the big metropolitan districts.

It is fairly generally recognized by those who have studied the problem, that there is a serious and irrational bias against public investment and consumption in America. It is a result of the combination of high-pressure salesmanship for private consumption and traditional suspicion against increasing public budgets. It cannot possibly correspond to what people would really prefer if they could as readily follow their impulses to buy the means of collective consumption as they can buy private consumers' goods, and if the former were equally well advertised.

The Identity of Two Goals

All these major reforms are clearly in the interest of social justice, interpreted in the American sense of the ideals of liberty and equality of opportunity. At the same time it is the thesis of this book that an orientation of American policy in the direction of such reforms is a precondition for an expansion of the American economy that is not only rapid but steady. *Never in the history of America has there been a greater and more complete identity between the ideals of social justice and the requirements of economic progress.* The latter goal is not attainable if large-scale policy measures are not inaugurated to reach the former goal.

We are here discussing American social and economic policies from the point of view of their internal effects within the country. But we should not hide from ourselves that they have international implications in addition to those analyzed in Part II.

America will continue to reveal its defects in well publicized literature and films. This frankness is, and has always been, the strength of this great democracy. It is rooted in a sense of strength, and it gives further strength. But only as long as it is also made clear that America is earnestly laboring to overcome its defects.

What has impressed the world more than the very inferior status still inflicted on the Negroes in America is the fact that such serious efforts have been directed to improving that status—legally, politically, socially and economically—and that there has also been such a marked improvement since the beginning of the Second World War.

I can myself testify from two continents on which I happened to travel when the tragic Little Rock events occurred, and from my reading newspapers from a third, that what impressed the world more than the resistance against school integration in Arkansas and the undignified way of doing it was that the courts stood firm, as did the United States government. America is not South Africa.

But a prerequisite is that the situation be dynamic, that things happen and that they move in the right direction. In the longer run it detracts from the position of the United States as leader in the Western world if it leaves its cities blighted by vast horrible slums, if in international comparisons it lags behind in social security for its old people, its invalids, its widows, and its children, and if generally it accepts so much abject poverty for a large

part of the nation. The relative economic stagnation in
America, closely related to social inequality as rapid progress would be to increasing equality, cannot be permitted
for long to be what characterizes the United States.

None is watched so suspiciously as the one who is
rising. None has so little license, needs all his virtue
so much as the leader. And America for its own security cannot retreat from leadership.*

A Necessary Qualification and a Negative Inference

Our reasoning up to this point has proceeded without
taking into consideration what is politically feasible in
present-day America. The conclusions we have reached
are objective in the sense that they logically follow as in-
ferences from the facts as we see them, together with the
premises of the American ideals of economic progress,
liberty, and equality of opportunity. It does not follow,
however, that they are realistic in the sense that they will
easily and rapidly lead to political action.

To the problem of the political inhibitions to rationality
I shall devote Chapter 7. At this point, it only remains to
state a negative inference, which is also logically founded.
If our analysis is correct and the following propositions
are accepted:

that unemployment and underemployment in America
are increasingly becoming structural;

that, therefore, a readjustment of the quality of the labor supply to fit the labor demand is a condition for full
employment;

* *An American Dilemma,* p. 1020.

that this readjustment requires large-scale policy efforts in the field of education, training, and retraining;

that, in their turn, such efforts in order not to be wasted and ineffective presuppose forceful efforts to eradicate poverty;

that rapid and steady growth of the economy in the present stage of technological development also requires the mobilization of the vast unmet needs among the poor and in the public sector in order to stabilize aggregate demand on a high and rising level;

that the surplus of manual labor released by technical development in agriculture and manufacturing industry, even if decreased by this increase of aggregate demand, must be re-employed by means of a vast increase of construction work of various sorts, which at the same time raises a need for retraining and implies the satisfaction of unmet needs;

then it is also clear that blocking these reforms, or pursuing them on a smaller scale or less rapidly than required, will result in a failure to realize rapid and at the same time steady growth and to reach a full-employment economy.

A boom, in whatever way induced, will then soon be broken by a new recession without ever having risen to the level of full utilization of productive resources and, in particular, of the labor force. As a trend, rising unemployment levels would then still prevail.

CHAPTER 5

The Problems of Inflation and the Balancing of Foreign Exchange

A "Balanced Budget" and a Balanced Economy

LEAVING for the moment the central problem of what particular demands should be increased, and assuming only that the government accepts a primary responsibility to create such conditions for business by its fiscal policy that production will expand, the means for increasing the aggregate demand must be decreased taxation and/or increased public expenditures. The budget—however we define that concept, and there are several possibilities—will then not be "balanced" in the American sense of the term.

At least at the start of an expansionist policy this is clear. Whether it also holds good in later years is more uncertain. It has recently been argued that the strengthening and broadening of the basis of taxation which will follow from economic expansion will later result in a balanced budget, perhaps even at lower rates of taxation.

This reasoning is of doubtful validity for several reasons. For one thing it assumes that a high growth rate is maintained over the years. Otherwise a new recession will again prevent balancing the budget.

It is, moreover, the thesis of this book that economic expansion which is not just rapid but steady is only possible if huge reforms are made in the interest of social justice. Otherwise it will be impossible to maintain a steady rise of total demand, and the supply of labor will not be fitted to the demand for labor. The induced expansion will soon turn into a new recession. The reforms will necessarily imply very substantial increases in public expenditures. Even taking into account the higher yields of taxation at given rates of taxation, a balanced budget might then have to imply higher rates. The citizens affected by such increases in their taxation could nevertheless be better off after taxation, because of the effects of economic expansion on their individual incomes.

But this whole way of stating the fiscal problem in terms of balancing the budget does not strike at what is relevant from the point of view of economic policy. Indeed, *the concept of a "balanced budget" in which taxation pays for all public expenditures, independently of the character and incidence of the many different items of taxation and of expenditures, is an irrational construct,* which is nowadays given significance only in American discussion, popular and political.

What really matters is not a "balanced budget" but a "balanced economy." In different settings—dependent among other things on the size and character of both taxes and public expenditures—and in different conjunctures a balanced economy may require an "overbalanced," a "balanced," or an "underbalanced" budget. It is encouraging that rational ideas of functional finance are increasingly accepted not only by the administration but by the business community in America.

But it is in itself important that such a large number of American voters and responsible politicians still think in terms of "balancing" the budget, and that almost all of them support it when referring to what should be accomplished over a number of years. It very much increases the difficulties of getting the American people and the Congress to accept the policy measures that are needed in order to set the American economy firmly into a pattern of rapid and steady growth.

One particular effect of the lingering idea that balancing the budget is the right thing to strive for can be seen now when the United States for the first time in its history, at the initiative of President Kennedy, is trying to accelerate economic growth through the deliberate creation of a deficit in the federal budget by means of decreased taxation. Not only are voices heard to suggest that the decreases in taxation should be matched by decreases in expenditures. Most or all of those who do not share this view still see in the deficit they are intent upon creating a reason to be particularly cautious in letting expenditures rise. This attitude is irrational and defeats the longer-range aim of the tax reductions. If it is true that a rapid and steady growth of the American economy cannot be assured except by huge reforms requested also in the interest of social justice which mostly imply large expenditures from the federal budget, this is an irrefutable logical inference.

The Risk of Inflation

A risk, however, is that the expansionist policies might unbalance the economy. This is a different thing and a real danger. These policies might overstimulate investments, generally or in certain fields, so that after a short time the result is an inflationary development that may go so far and proceed so fast that sooner or later it has to be broken by inducing a recession. This is contrary to the goal of public policy that economic growth should be not only rapid but steady.

To accomplish that objective will require careful planning and the availability of flexible means for controlling the volume of consumption, production and, in particular, investment. I cannot go into these problems in detail in this brief book and have to restrict myself to making a few observations.

To begin with, we should realize that general monetary controls are clumsy and largely ineffective, particularly in the short run. The long-term rate of interest in a rapidly expanding economy should be kept on a fairly stable level. But this should not exclude a wider utilization of discriminatory controls of the money and capital market on strategic points, for instance on credits for home construction or for installment buying. But in the main the short-term controls have to be sought in the fiscal field.

The important thing about the fiscal controls of economic development is that, since the problem is how to reach a balance on a high level of economic activity, the controls will have to be applied on short notice. Even if ideally they could be thought of as automatic, reacting to changes in certain indices, such automatism can hardly be based on sufficiently and rapidly analyzable statistical material even in a country like the United States with an excellent statistical service that is also kept relatively very up-to-date. At least until our economic planning has been perfected—as discussed in the next chapter—there remains a large element of judgment that must be applied. The needed short-term flexibility of the fiscal controls must be provided by the Congress giving the Executive a leeway for quick changes of various taxes and expenditures and, particularly, for changing their timing.

In various countries a large arsenal of such flexible fiscal controls have been tested out, and more will be invented in the near future. To this potential arsenal belongs the Swedish system of allowing industry to set aside tax-free reserves which can only be utilized for investment by a decision of the government. Other possibilities are special taxes on investment in general or investment in particular fields, and on consumption or particular types of consumption, which are adjustable or applied only after government decision. Allowances for capital depreciation as well as the expenditures for advertising could be made adjustable. The timing of public expenditures already decided upon, particularly of the investment type, is also one of the fiscal policy levers available.

It is fairly certain that in the future these matters will increasingly be studied scientifically at our universities and research institutions. The government will also increasingly be pressed to consider how such flexible fiscal controls can be put into practice as it really comes to grip with the big problem of keeping the economy expanding rapidly while avoiding such warping and twisting in the economy which would necessitate a recession.

This is, however, mainly a vision of the future, though some idea of it should be present for those who plan economic policy for the United States today. Thinking more specifically of the present situation, two points need to be made. The first one is that higher capacity utilization, following a more rapid growth, will tend to lower costs which should counteract inflationary tendencies. It should also be noted that inflation is systematically overstated in the statistics by not allowing for quality improvements and innovations. We know from recent experiences in many countries that there is no close relation between the rate of growth and the rate of inflation. Much depends upon how balanced is the manner in which growth proceeds. Prices may rise while the economy is lagging; they may be pushed upwards by expansion though the expansion is limited to only a sector of the economy. And prices may remain steady though the economy as a whole is expanding.

The second point is that the effects, socially and otherwise, of the low and unstable rate of growth of the American economy are so serious that honesty demands that I should frankly state that I would be prepared to take a moderate rise in the price level, perhaps even 2 or 3 per cent annually, if that should be the condition for economic growth. I believe that most people, if they really thought the problem through, would agree with me.

But that choice may not be open. In order to decide on this point we need first to consider the United States balance of payment situation.

Foreign Exchange Difficulties

During President Eisenhower's second term the fear of losing more gold and incurring more short-term foreign liabilities was a powerful reason for not venturing on an expansionist policy aimed at getting the American economy going at full speed. Even the Kennedy government feels the United States international balance of payment situation as a serious restraint on its freedom to move ahead.

There are reasons to question whether too much consideration is not given to this restraint. If the American economy were set on the road to rapid growth, this would by itself change anticipations in the United States and abroad. Americans would be less interested in seeking outlets for investment in other countries. At the same time foreigners would be induced to invest more in American securities to share in American economic progress. Undoubtedly, part of the present situation in the United States is the result of a vicious circle. Anxiety about its international balance of payments and particularly about the drain on its gold reserves has induced the United States to be satisfied with the relative economic stagnation that itself is a main reason for the flight of capital from the United States.

A depreciation of the dollar in terms of gold cannot be a way out of the difficulties. For one thing it goes against the nation's pride. It would, moreover, imply giving a bonus mainly to South Africa and the Soviet Union, which are the main gold producers. This is hardly apt to make such a policy attractive to the United States. As a means of improving the competitive position of the United States it is also not very effective, since such a move would probably be followed in many, if not most, other countries.

It is much less feasible to reach international adjustment by means of changing the rate of foreign exchange for a big country like the United States than for a smaller one. On the other hand, the size of the United States and the fact that exports and imports form a much smaller part of its national product should also make it possible to plan its internal economic policy with less immediate consideration of the effects on the exchange situation.

The question can then be raised whether there is not in the United States—as, indeed, in other countries—an irrational fixation on the importance of preserving a big gold reserve and on not using it as a reserve which should be expendable. If this fixation could be loosened, the general exchange situation in the world would be improved.

Keeping to the United States exchange situation, this question can be made more concrete. If legal and other restrictions were lifted and gold then started to move abroad even somewhat faster than now, would it really matter? Would not enough gold soon come back—under the two conditions, *nota bene*, that the American economy had begun to expand rapidly and that the cost and price structure was not getting out of hand. To the latter condition we will come back in the next section.

Who could be eager to accumulate more gold? There is some private gold hoarding and it could become accelerated. But it can hardly be a question of large demands. In regard to public authorities, Britain and the underdeveloped countries cannot afford to increase their gold holdings much if at all. Would not even France and Germany, which unlike the United States and Britain have enjoyed rapid economic growth and have been stacking up gold reserves, soon find that they have invested too much of their liquid assets in ways that do not pay any interest? And if these two and some other countries would be just a little obedient to old theory and let the bigger gold reserves lead to an increased credit volume and higher levels of costs and prices, this would be favorable for the United States balance of trade and payments and, more generally, work for improved international monetary balance. Such a movement towards overexpansion, incidentally, seems well on the way for some time.

This assumes, of course, that foreign governments and particularly those having large liquid assets of dollars would not participate in, or permit, a run on gold. They have very important interests of their own in not doing so and there is a strong basis of interest solidarity behind the co-operation of central banks. If the American government wanted to be more firmly assured against a run on its gold, it could moreover give a gold guarantee to those foreign central banks that keep liquid dollar reserves. It is fairly self-evident that the short-term interest in the United States should be made to move more independently from the long-term rate of interest, as is the case in other countries. In certain eventualities it may even be advisable to have special, higher interest rates for foreign capital, a device that has been used, though only in the other direction, by Switzerland and Germany.

The more basic problem is, of course, to reach a more perfect organization of the international money market. When the two countries which provide the world with international currency, the United States and Great Britain, have been forced into deflationary policies at home, which are now endangering the stability of economic growth everywhere and not least in the underdeveloped countries, this is basically the same problem which my late teacher, friend, and predecessor at Stockholm University, Gustav Cassel, wrestled with after the First World War. Politically he was anything but an irresponsible radical, and I feel comforted in recalling that my views stated above are not basically different from his of forty years ago.

Like him, I am aware that this problem can be solved in many alternative ways. And, like him, I would give preference to a simple solution, calling for a minimum of institutional changes, as it is always difficult to reach international agreement on beautifully perfected but complicated schemes for international co-operation. This we should be aware of after the stillbirth of the International Trade Organization which received such extensive prenatal care, and after we have seen the International Monetary Fund taking a far more modest responsibility than was initially planned and anticipated.

Meanwhile we should be aware that America's national policies are of crucial importance even for the international organization of the money market. America should lead the world in more generous international fiscal arrangements just as in economic growth rates.

The Price and Cost Structure

When all this is said, it nevertheless remains true that the United States cannot in the somewhat longer run preserve the international payment position it needs to meet its foreign military and civilian obligations, though it runs a foreign trade surplus of several billion dollars, if its price and cost structure moves up faster than in other countries. That has not been the case in recent years and it does not correspond to the present trend. Even were a more rapid growth of the American economy induced, there are, as I mentioned, economies in achieving fuller utilization of capacity. And the changed anticipations, steering the capital flows, to which I also referred above, should afford considerable leeway.

Nevertheless, the cost and price structure has to be watched carefully. The United States government may have to extend its control over prices and over labor costs as a consequence of its determination to induce a considerably more rapid and also steady growth.

In regard to price control, I have often asked myself whether the American government, which for decades and generations has fought monopoly with such courage and sometimes vehemence by means of legislation and court action and yet failed to prevent a continuous concentration of market power and the transformation of crucial prices into "administered prices," should not now be prepared to tone down its rather fruitless fight against monopoly but instead ask for a share in controlling administered prices which are so decisive for the general trend of prices. President Kennedy's dramatic action in preventing steel prices from rising a year ago and his more cautiously expressed anxiety this spring about their increase may in the long historical view come to stand as a harbinger of things to come.

For a long time, there has been greater interest in demanding more government control of wages and in preventing the major labor conflicts that so frequently occur in the United States. The principles that wage levels as well as other conditions for employment should be left to collective bargaining of the partners in the labor market and that the rights to call a strike or declare a lockout belong to the liberties which cannot be given up in a free economy are, however, so well established in America, that, as yet, government interference in the labor market has been unplanned, infrequent, and hesitating.

I think we should face the problem whether more government regulations in the labor market, more of direct intervention in the bargaining and, at the same time, some form of price control may not be a necessary consequence of an economic policy directed towards rapid and steady growth in the United States.

In the Labor Market

In regard to this problem, reference is more and more often made to Sweden. In Sweden a situation has been reached where the bargaining process regularly leads to agreements. No open labor conflicts of importance have occurred in recent years, and it is confidently expected that none will occur. The government is keeping away from direct interference in the labor market. And Sweden has a full employment economy.

The agreements as such may on the whole be considered satisfactory to the public interest. Generally, they are directed at preventing both excessive wage rises in certain sectors and too low wages in others and, with qualification, at preventing the general level from rising too fast. When that level has nevertheless been rising faster than productivity, causing an inflationary trend of prices, this has its explanation primarily in the keen competition among employers in a full employment economy which causes them to overbid each other. About half of the rise in wages has been what in Sweden is called the "wage-drift" above the agreed wages. The system has thus not been an unqualified success insofar as stabilizing the cost structure is concerned. The best that can be said is that the Swedish organization of the labor market is preventing conflicts and that the two organizations in co-operation are doing their part to prevent a cost-push inflation.

It is useful in this context to point out the conditions which have led to this fortunate situation. Almost all workers are organized, not by compulsion but because it has become a matter of course like many other things in society. The unions are open in principle and also rather generally in practice. They are democratically governed with a fairly high degree of active participation on the part of the members in running them. The unions are for the most part industrial and not split according to craft. Considerable power is vested in the central organization of all unions, articulating the common interest of all workers. The employers, on their side, are organized in a parallel way. All legal conflicts concerning the interpretation of contract obligations are brought to a special court presided over by a high-level judge, while representatives of the employers and the employees serve as assessors. The practice of collective bargaining has over the years developed into a very serious but basically friendly exercise. The officials of the two organizations feel close to each other and they and their constituent members have gradually matured to the degree that in co-operation they serve, and know that they serve, as *de facto* agencies for public policy.

Such an order in the labor market is not more than a remote possibility in America, and many believe that it will never be reached. It is also fairly unique among the other rich countries. In many of them, for instance in Australia, there is a regularized system for government intervention, substituting to a larger or a smaller degree for genuine collective bargaining. In Denmark, otherwise so similar to Sweden, every threatening big labor conflict automatically becomes a political issue in which the government and parliament have the last say. As the parties to an incipient conflict know this, and as one or the other party tends to feel that the political settlement will be in its favor, this works to frustrate collective bargaining. Britain, on the other hand, is not very much better off than the United States. Only about half of the workers are organized, to a large extent in craft unions of which many specialize in very disturbing nuisance strikes not authorized by any central union authority.

I have always seen good reasons for legislation about the constitution and functioning of the trade unions, guaranteeing their openness to new members, proper accounting of their finances, and full democracy in their government. I have seen it as a major misfortune that legislation about trade unions has so often been considered a reactionary cause in the United States and has put the liberals up in arms to defend their freedom. I will permit myself to quote with my full concurrence a statement made long ago by that rightly respected radical, Norman Thomas, who cannot be considered a foe of workers' rights:

> Briefly, I propose that every union, to be entitled to recognition as the agency of the workers in collective bargaining (and without that recognition most unions would be doomed), must conform to certain minimum standards of democracy. Its doors must be open to all qualified workers, regardless of race, creed, or color, under reasonable standards of initiation fees and dues. Next, its constitution, by-laws, and practices must provide for orderly elections at reasonable intervals. And finally, a disciplinary procedure must be set up which will protect members of the union from arbitrary punishment more serious than most judges and juries can impose. Possibly some other requirements might be laid down, for instance, with regard to votes on strikes, but those which I have mentioned seem to me essential.*

Many of these demands have now been realized, though some are left unmet or have not become effective. The good unions which represent the great majority of unionized labor have nothing to fear from that type of legislation.

In the present context, the question of direct intervention in the labor market is more important. That the United States needs legislation, and considerably widened legislation, on minimum wages for the large unorganized sectors of the economy as long as they are unorganized is

* "How Democratic are Labor Unions?" *Harper's Magazine* (May 1942), pp. 655-662.

clear. This is direct intervention, though exerted through legislation.

But the really crucial question is whether the United States can attain success of policy aimed at much more rapid and at the same time steady economic growth without taking measures to prevent the outbreak of devastating labor conflicts and also prevent excessive wage increases in certain small craft unions, that can exploit their power to put a halt to big enterprises. Much more important than these two interests is, however, the need to prevent too rapid increases in wages in the few strategic industries in America whose prices are particularly important for the general price level.

In recent years, wages in these industries have not risen in proportion to productivity in America, which reflects the high level of unemployment that has weakened the trade unions and at the same time contributed to the lag in consumer demand that is a basic factor behind the low economic growth rate. Economic expansion and a high level of employment could be expected to make cost-push inflation more of a reality than it has been up till now. As these industries have administered prices and are often easily able to accommodate union demands, and as their unions usually are relatively strong, their wages —and prices—may in a more rapidly expanding economy be expected to rise faster than is compatible with long-range international exchange stability.

Even apart from the fact that this danger is partly due to these industries having administered prices, it is difficult to conceive of democratic America applying wage controls without also controlling prices and profits. Compared with a country with a more complete and perfect organization in the labor market, the United States may thus be under the compulsion to deviate further from *laissez faire* in compensating for deficiencies in its institutional infrastructure. It has, as a matter of fact, already had to do this, as shown by the minimum wage legislation and many other acts of legislation and administration relating to the labor market.

To these problems I will return in Chapter 7. The one remark I would like to add here is that it would naturally be very much more desirable and very much more in accordance with American ideals if instead the workers' organizations in the labor market could grow and improve rapidly, and if, at the same time, the employers could be similarly organized in genuine employers' federations, and if on both sides their thinking and practices could become so much more responsible that a properly balanced system of organization in the labor market could increasingly be a *de facto* agency for public policy, relieving the government of the necessity of intervention, at least to an extent.

CHAPTER 6

Long-Range Economic Planning

The Need for Long-Range Planning

ONCE America has decided that it wants to inaugurate a policy leading to rapid and steady economic growth, this implies the necessity of long-range economic planning. It is not possible rationally just to want economic growth. There will always be questions to answer: growth *of what* and *for what,* and growth *at what cost*—in the latter respect, not only economically but in terms of changing institutions and human relations in case they do not all go in the desired direction and are not part of the growth that is aimed at.

The demand for long-range planning has particular force and gets a particular twist if a high growth rate is to be maintained through time so that a boom shall not end in another recession. The reason is that there are certain fundamental relations in society that must be adjusted by intentional government policy if a high rate of expansion is to continue unbroken. That adjustment does not occur automatically, simply because a spurt to business is provided.

We have in this book pointed to the need of radical improvement of the quality of labor that is unemployed or not productively employed, and we have stressed how this, in its turn, necessitates huge investments in education, training, and retraining of workers, and how such investments to be effective and not wasteful have to be given the frame of a general attack on poverty. We have pointed to the urgent need of creating a demand for released manual labor in many types of construction work. We have also shown that in the present stage of technological development the needs of the poor have to be changed into effective demand to provide a rising aggregate demand as a reliable basis for a long-range expansion of production. We have emphasized that in a full employment economy the price and cost structure has to be stabilized in order to preserve a balanced exchange position without which expansion will soon have to be stopped.

These various strands of government policy do not fall into place in the big puzzle without detailed planning in all the various fields: public construction work, spatial and vocational reallocation of the labor force, education, training and retraining, social security of different types, changed taxation on the federal, state, and municipal level, agricultural policy, wage and price policies, and so on. New drafts of city plans and transport systems have to be produced.

But the main thing in long-range planning is that all these technical plans have to be integrated into an over-all plan for the development of the economy as a whole. That over-all plan, indicating not only the speed but also the main direction of economic growth, is needed for framing government policy. It is equally needed as a basis for planning in private business, which otherwise has to operate with a complex of important parameters only in the form of guesses, founded on no real knowledge.

What Long-Range Economic Planning Is

Long-range economic planning has to proceed in two stages.

What is first needed are comprehensive *forecasts* of what on different assumptions will happen to the American economy in five, ten, and twenty years' time. The fact that there are interrelations among the various factors—as there are in a population forecast between births, deaths, age structure, and population increase—is the reason why such prognoses make real contributions to knowledge. Economic forecasts should be worked out for alternative rates of growth and different patterns of growth. The high level of econometric expertness in America and the perfection of the electronic computing machines make it feasible to work out such models with much more specificity and exactitude than only a few years ago.

These alternative forecasts spell out what is possible, what is necessary in order to reach and maintain a certain rate of growth following a certain pattern of direction, and what it implies in terms of employment and the movement of people, educational efforts, investment in various fields, and of everything else.

The second stage of planning then becomes the intentional *choice* between the open possibilities, taking account of what the nation wants to achieve, what policy means are available for the government, what policy means the government is prepared to use, and how it is prepared to use them. It can not be rationally entered upon except on the basis of earlier forecasts giving knowledge about fundamental causal relations. The second stage, on the other hand, is implied already in the first and forecasting stage, as the forecasts cannot be made out of the blue, without some general assumptions of the type of economic development aimed at. But this is true only to a limited extent, within which *forecasting is a purely technical and scientific exercise.*

This may sound simple and encouraging. The reasons for my deep misgivings at having to urge more and better planning upon the United States as it now consciously heads towards attempting to have a more rapid and steadier economic growth are discussed in the next chapter. It should be stressed here, however, that my misgivings apply only to what has been referred to above as the second stage of long-range planning. To carry out the studies in the first stage is a simpler thing and an obvious duty of our profession. Its only effects on government and business must be to make it possible for them to become more rational in the way in which their decisions shape the future.

Long-range planning has to be done on a national level and Washington has, of course, a primary responsibility. But there is no reason why it should not be a concern even of the great American universities and other independent research institutions.

To begin with, however, it is a duty of some government agencies. We can ask if the law has not actually directed the President's Council of Economic Advisers to supervise exactly such forecasting, preparing the ground for rational policy decisions. In any case, the duty is implicit in its general directives. From the special point of view of labor utilization the Department of Labor, the Department of Health, Education and Welfare, and the new Department for Urban Affairs, which the President has proposed but not as yet got Congress to accept, and naturally also the Departments of Commerce and the Treasury—all should have a primary interest in this type of forecasting and programming.

Perhaps it should be pointed out that rational long-range planning is, of course, much easier for a big country like the United States whose foreign relations are less important for its economy, than for a small country. We can see this by thinking how very much more difficult it would be to make a reliable forecast of the economic development for Wisconsin than for the United States as a whole.

Why America Is Lagging in Long-Range Economic Planning

America as a civilization has its interests focused upon the immediate, the concrete, and the experimental in a remarkable way. In all the sciences, including the social ones, America has always had to rely upon European thought for philosophy and theory, for the comprehensive grip of things and events, and for the long view. In recent time and in economics, Keynes is an outstanding example, as is Schumpeter, who even permitted himself to be imported to the country.

The American people senses drama in what actually happens. This is why the air is always so laden with excitement in America and why every visit to this country becomes such a very pleasant, inspiring, and stimulating experience to a visitor. But this cultural trait of America is not conducive to long-range economic planning.

Among the things that have not changed in America and specifically in Washington during different administrations is what from the point of view of the problems here under discussion must appear as a general tendency to nearsightedness among both politicians and experts; I noted this twenty years ago.* There are today an astonishing number of competent people who can offhand give

* *An American Dilemma* (New York, Harper, 1944), p. 719.

a detailed and comprehensive analysis in quantitative terms of what is just now happening, how all important economic indices have recently been moving, and how they are likely to move in the months ahead.

Everybody is intensively interested in what is going to happen next, who is in and who is out, who is behind whom or against whom, and who thinks what. This is also what Washington reporting in the press and the periodicals is about. In regard to economic development an altogether excessive interest is attached to when the next recession or the next upturn of business is going to occur. I will confess that not even as a shareholder do I take much interest in this sort of pastime, since I have neither the inclination nor the time to speculate.

But this general attitude is adverse to long-range planning. Even at the universities and other research institutions studies in terms of the long-range future are neglected, except in regard to population and resources. Not only the President and Congress but also leaders in business are left without that intellectualized vision of what the future holds in store in regard to the economic development in more general terms. But such a vision is needed for rational decision, particularly when it implies investment or other actions which have consequences far ahead, as have most legislation about taxes, tariffs, and everything else.

It is difficult to avoid the reflection that the neglect by government agencies as well as by American universities and other research institutions of the long-range prospects of the American economy as a whole and the undue concentration on short-range issues—or at the nongovernmental institutions often on timeless and by any standards less important terminological questions and unworldly constructs—is partly responsible for the failure of my distinguished and numerous fellow economists to disseminate more economic understanding among the American people, in spite of the fact that America for such a long time had a wider college attendance than any other Western country. Commonly held less-enlightened views on budget balancing and the role of gold in the monetary system are cases in point.

When America is less advanced in long-range economic planning, this can, however, not entirely be explained as a reflection of a cultural trait, even if this general conditioning of the Americans should not be forgotten. It is obvious that one important cause is an intensive lack of interest, to put it euphemistically, by the business community that is so powerful in America.

This attitude taken by business would seem to be irrational. For one thing, a long-range grasp of whither the American economy as a whole is heading is essential for its own planning. The lag in long-range national planning represents, as already pointed out, a missing complex of parameters for rational decision-making in business as well as in government.

In America long-range planning still has a Russian and Communist smell to many. But attempts at that type of forecasting and programming are rapidly becoming a regular duty of most governments in the Western world.

French planning has recently had much publicity in America of an astonishingly sympathetic sort, explainable perhaps because the French political regime seems to be conservative. French planning, however, has a particularly strong bias towards "dirigism"—or what Americans would call regimentation—made possible by a large nationalized sector in industry and especially banking. The "dirigism" is implemented by a rather intensive central control of investments through the consolidation of the power of financing. I doubt whether, after a closer look, American business would find the French type of planning particularly congenial, except perhaps by some who have a positive appreciation of the fact that neither popular organizations nor parliament has much of a say in it.

But there are other countries where planning takes less of a "dirigist" form and leaves greater role for free adjustment of private business after a much smaller public sector has been more carefully planned on the basis of long-range forecasting. Sweden and Norway have perhaps advanced furthest, both scientifically and practically. But even Great Britain is beginning to try its hand at this new art. Under a Tory government that country has recently been weary and wobbling in its economic policies—though with much basic strength, founded upon the solid quality of its technicians, its research people, and not least, its officials, and upon the traditions and common sense of its people at large. There is emerging a sort of national agreement, shared by the Tories and definitely by the business community, that to solve its problems Britain needs to join the countries attempting long-range economic planning.

In America such a unity of views does not, as yet, exist. Business leaders and other conservatively inclined people fear that the provision of the alternative set of forecasts, which above was called the first stage of long-range economic planning, will be dangerous. It might tempt the government to meddle more in business—and actually give it good reasons to do so.

There is undoubtedly a rational foundation for this apprehension and we should not conceal it. But is not its translation into a fear irrational and out of step with the needs of the time? The bearing of the whole argument in this book is that without the government taking on greatly increased responsibilities there is little hope of getting America to become again a country with a progressive economy, and of saving America from serious damage both to its power in foreign relations and to the internal unity of the nation.

To attempt to give the government a greater role in the economy without utilizing the superb intellectual resources which America possesses and now disperses on tasks of much lesser importance would be part of the waste in this country of abundance of resources.

Work on long-term forecasts and programs would also have a wider educational function in America, besides giving the needed basis for rational policy formation in government and business. Only by writing on the wall in definite and concrete figures the opportunities that could be realized by a change in policies can America be made to wake up to its old ambitions and new necessities.

I am afraid that the resistance of prejudice and vested interests, mostly misunderstood, will postpone this awakening and that the development in the years to come will be a checkered one. The more important is it then not to leave unutilized this powerful means of gradually educating the general public to a more rational understanding of America's economic problems. Education has in America's whole history been the major hope for improving the individuals and society. Not least on this score do I share American ideals and hopes.

CHAPTER 7

Government and Participation of the People in Government

The Need for a Bigger Role for the Government

FOLLOWING the outline for this little book I have tried to reason logically from what I believe are the facts and what I know are the American ideals about how their society should be. On this basis I have presented challenges and urged reforms.

I have taken only scant considerations to what is politically feasible in present-day America. Incidentally, I think this is how the economist should act in the first place when he aspires to advise the government and the people. He decreases his usefulness in the field of his primary competence when right at the start he accepts as his own all the inhibitions against following reason which the politicians are laboring under.

But in the end any realistic analysis will also have to consider the established patterns and inherent predilections of the political system which is assumed to meet these challenges and inaugurate these reforms.

Any move towards a planned achievement of these reforms will imply a "bigger government in a sense." As a matter of fact, the trend towards big government has prevailed for a long time, as everybody should know. The

United States has moved far on the road towards the welfare state, though as yet not so far as some of the most advanced of the other rich countries. There is an immense and continually growing amount of public interference in the economy, conditioning it and redirecting it. There is, indeed, as in other rich countries, a widely dispersed system of "economic planning" of a pragmatic and, as yet, largely unco-ordinated type.

What is now becoming an urgent necessity in America is in the first place a much better co-ordination of already existing government policies, *i.e.* their integration into a more perfect, deliberate, and rational long-range planning. This is what is implied in what was referred to in the last chapter as the second stage of planning.

As a result of this planning and co-ordination it would certainly be possible to scrap a lot of specific regulations and policy interventions which have spuriously grown up *ad hoc*. They would be replaced by more general regulations. Indeed, successful planning should free the citizens from a lot of nuisance public intervention of which there is an astonishing amount in the United States. *Planning does not mean more detailed controls but more over-all direction on the part of the national community of which all citizens are a part.**

I have referred to a bigger role for government, but by this I do not mean a bigger bureaucracy. I find American government offices appallingly big in relation to the functions they perform. And many functions themselves would disappear in a more perfect planning.*

At the same time there is bound to be a bigger government in the sense that the government will have to take increased responsibility for organizing public consumption in the fields of education and health. It will have to redistribute incomes on a large scale by its taxation, so-

* This thought and my general views on planning as largely a relaxation of detailed controls are further developed in *Beyond the Welfare State* (New Haven, Yale University Press, 1960); see particularly pp. 88-99 and about the American situation pp. 99-102.

cial security schemes, and agricultural policies. It will
have to invest much more in slum clearance and low-
rent housing and, indeed, in the complete renewal of the
cities and their transport systems, as well as more generally in resource development. It will generally have to
increase its responsibilities for a larger part of consumption and investment and, consequently, for employment
and production. And all this activity of the bigger government must be co-ordinated under the aspects of the con-
verging ideals of greater social justice and a more rapid
and steady expansion of the economy.

These conclusions, the reasons for which have been
presented in the earlier chapters, are apt to fill good Americans and friendly foreign observers with forebodings that
the American people may have to go through severe crises
before they really come to grips with the task of enlarging
and improving their government.

Speaking for myself, study and experience have made
me realize what an exceedingly difficult task government
planning and an expansion of its responsibilities is in any
country, even when the preconditions for social and economic engineering are very much more favorable than
they are for the time being in the United States.

For this reason, I would never suggest government intervention except when necessary for the pursuance of
really important interests and ideals. I would always feel
deeply satisfied if things were to take care of themselves.
In choosing means for government conditioning of the
economy, I would always prefer the most general, the
least specific ones, implying a minimum of discretionary
power for administrators. Whenever I could work the controls simply by an adjustment of prices, I would find this
highly advantageous.

For reasons of both efficiency and democracy, I would
prefer decentralization, pushing the actual business of
regulatory intervention down to state, district, and local
authorities where it could be controlled as effectively as
possible by elected assemblies. Organizations in the in-

stitutional infrastructure, provided that they are reasonably well balanced, could also function together as agencies through bargaining and co-operation for public policy without direct government interference.

It is a very long time since I looked with any glee or exhilaration to the prospect that technological change and other fundamental changes in our national communities and in the world would force us to plan and control our economic life ever more intensely through the means of government. In the United States, more particularly, there are a number of reasons why the government and the administration cannot be expected to perform their tasks very effectively, especially if these tasks are rapidly widened.

The lack of a parliamentary cabinet government, assuring an automatic synchronization of the political will of the Executive and the Congress, too often leads to deadlocks. For the same reason, legislation in the United States is ordinarily not prepared with the care desirable for planning and co-ordination of government policies. Draft bills also run bigger risks of either not being enacted at all or enacted in an ill-considered and distorted form. The working rules of Congress are irrational to an extent which is astonishing in modern, efficient America.

A number of customs and patterns, having no basis whatsoever in the United States Constitution—for instance, the seniority rules for membership and, in particular, chairmanship of the committees of Congress and the extraordinary power awarded to their chairmen—strengthen these effects and specifically give greater power to reactionary and old men, often from the South that from an American point of view is culturally backward, and more generally, to the less enlightened forces.

The encouraging thing which I have seen happening is that many more responsible people today seriously discuss changes of these customs and patterns and even of the Constitution, which are no longer considered taboo as a generation ago. This implies a return to Thomas Jefferson's ideas of a continuously reformed constitution. But we should not expect rapid reforms.

There are similar shortcomings of the state governments of whom many, through extensive gerrymandering, have an overweight of reactionary representation from rural districts. This last deficiency may now be disappearing after the recent decisions of the United States Supreme Court, implying that equal representation means that representatives should have behind them as nearly equally numerous constituencies as practically possible. City governments have often been run by corrupt political machines, though in recent decades there have been great improvements.

Add to this that the considerable lag in the United States in the formation of an independent, nonpolitical civil service—and the competition for talent from business and universities—has implied that administrators on all levels have not generally acquired the security, responsibility, and efficiency that would be desired. Economic and social progress in America has had its origin much less in the activity of the administrators than in what was achieved on the farms, in the factories, in the business offices, and in the universities. At a juncture in American history when so much more will be requested from the government and the administration, this becomes a serious impediment.

In all these respects there have been great improvements. The reforms, however, have to be carried out concomitantly with a considerable enlargement of government activity. The United States is not in the same favorable position as Great Britain and Scandinavia. There the strong, efficient, and noncorrupt state was the creation of liberalism, when government activity was at a low point in the interlude between mercantilism and the modern welfare state.

This inheritance from the era of liberalism has, in those countries, meant a great deal in making the big government the success it has been. Nevertheless, it would be a far cry to say that even in those countries it has been anything like a complete success.

Lack of a Balanced Institutional Infrastructure

There is, moreover, in the United States a greater lack of democratic balance in the institutional infrastructure within the government apparatus than in those countries mentioned above that are most similar to America in fundamental ideals and ambitions. The situation in the labor market was touched upon in Chapter 5.

I should at this point mention that I would see nothing wrong, as such, in the organizational strength of American business, provided that it were only counterbalanced by equally strong and, above all, equally well spread out organizations of the people as workers and consumers. Nor should I have anything against strong organizations defending the interest of American agriculture if they were not so exclusively dominated by the big farmers, leaving the small farmers, the small tenants, and the workers without much of a voice.

The implication of all this is that *for the time being a much more than desirable share of responsibility, not only for the general direction but even for the execution of public policy, has to be carried by national and state governments, which themselves lack the structure that would make them ideally fitted for that task.* As already mentioned, the United States government is thus under the compulsion to deviate further from *laissez faire* in order to substitute by legislation and administrative acts for the largely nonexistent workers' and consumers' organizations and, consequently, the lack of a democratic balance in the institutional infrastructure. In many fields it has, indeed, already felt compelled to do it. Sweden needs of course no legislation on minimum wages, but the United States does.

Popular Participation

A basic cause of, or at least a common element in, all this is that the citizens' participation in public life, taken in its broadest terms, is lower in America than generally in countries that are most similar to it in basic values. This is true at elections but still more in the intervals between elections.

It is particularly true in regard to the organizations in the institutional infrastructure. When the great majority of workers are not unionized and when so relatively many unions are in the hands of petty dictators who often exploit their position, the explanation for this is, of course, that workers are not alert and enlightened enough to defend their interests by organizing themselves in unions or, when unionized, do not shoulder responsibility for their unions.

It is the poor people in America who are mute, inarticulate, and inactive to an extent that corresponding strata in the other advanced countries are not—with the result that they have not gotten a fair deal. They are now, as is clear from Chapters 2-4, facing the greatest dangers inherent in the present developments. They have the greatest interest in fundamental reforms and in pressing for them by active, continuing, and diversified participation in public affairs through all the agencies that democratic society allows. But in America self-generating interest organizations do not spring forward as a matter of course in these strata

The explanation of this relative lack of integration of the lower strata within the nation is not that America is young, as the popular view wants to have it. As Oscar Wilde said: "The youth of America is their oldest tradition. It has been going on now for three hundred years." America is, in fact, the oldest modern democracy in the world, having had universal suffrage from about the middle of the nineteenth century. Its great universities were founded in the era of the Renaissance as most of those in Europe. And, more specifically, its trade union movement is almost a hundred years older than that of the Scandinavian countries, where that movement has grown to such higher importance and to so much greater public responsibility.

Neither is the bigness of the country and the fact that for almost the whole of the nineteenth century the boundaries for its economics and social life were expanding out in the wilderness enough of an explanation. The New England communities were often quite well organized. The frontier communities early demonstrated valiant community efforts to stabilize law and order which were remarkable when we think of how difficult it must have been to keep an orderly life under extreme physical conditions. These things can not in any case explain the carelessness about local affairs demonstrated in so many stable townships and cities, small as well as big, often resulting in inefficient government, collusion, and corruption.

It is instead related to the fact of the nation's being composed of people stemming from different national cultures. I have no doubt that in time America will become a well integrated nation. I feel support for this hopeful opinion in the big changes I have witnessed since I first experienced America a whole generation ago.

But the further progress of national integration is bound to be a time-consuming and gradual growth process. In the present context this implies that much that in some other advanced countries can be safely delegated to local self-government and to the co-operation and bargaining between the organization in a well-balanced basic institutional infrastructure, will in America have to be done through direct controls by the central and state governments and their agencies.

Meanwhile, whatever can be done to strengthen popular participation and organizational activity on those lower levels should certainly be done. Everybody knows that this is in the cherished tradition of Thomas Jefferson, who wanted decentralization of power and responsibility to small units, and of all the other national heroes in the liberal tradition of America; I speak here not as an outsider but entirely within that great tradition. But it does not give much of an answer to America's immediate problem of applying social and economic engineering in a radical fashion in order to overcome the relative stagnation which is creeping upon its economy.

The Lively Participation by a Few

It would give an altogether too gloomy picture of present prospects in America if we did not supplement our observations on the lack of participation by the lower strata by pointing to the prevalence, on the other hand, of a much more intensive participation than elsewhere in the Western world of a few, and to the fact that relatively much of this participation is unselfish and idealistic to an extent that is also rather unique in the world.

Americans are described as "joiners," though it is not commonly pointed out that the opposite is true of the lower strata. Much of this "joining" is for good causes.

And there is in America more than in any other country I know a particularly lively discussion of all issues and an eagerness to do what can be done in order to improve society and, indeed, the world. This is a Puritan and moralistic trait explainable by America's unique history. It is true that this holds good only in the higher strata. But it means that the interests of the poor will never lack their pleaders. If they can be lifted from apathy they will always have leaders. This becomes particularly important when the interests of the poor become so clearly identical with the interests of the whole nation.

The recent arguments about conformity in America are overworked in my opinion. There is unfortunately much more conformity in Sweden, and in Sweden the trend might be to increased conformity. America has still more than any other country I know a government through discussion. By that I mean that issues are argued and that this has influence upon what is done. If the masses of people can be induced to participate more intensely in the molding of their nation's and their own destiny, and if the freedom and the serious engagement in the public issues of the few can be preserved, I foresee a good, indeed extraordinarily good, future for America. I have never belonged to those who from time to time have foreseen that "it can happen here," meaning the faltering of democracy in America.

Twenty years ago I noted both the passivity of the masses in America and the equally astonishing liveliness among the upper strata, a situation which, in particular, took its expression in the common pattern of craving for "leadership" but also in accepting leadership to an extraordinary degree, matters which, at that time at least, were not much discussed but which I had to find out for myself. I may at this point perhaps refer in particular to Chapter 33 in *An American Dilemma* for a fuller development of the ideas in the two last sections and quote a few lines, which also point towards the future:

> Cultural fragmentation, the division of interest of the lower classes, and their loss of leaders, thus stamped the masses with inertia. They are accustomed to being static and receptive. They are not

daring, but long for security. They do not know how to cooperate and how to pool risks and sacrifices for a common goal. They do not meet much. They do not organize. They do not speak for themselves: they are the listeners in America. . . . Generally speaking, the lower classes in America have been inarticulate and powerless.

This is the more striking when the lower classes are compared with the "Pullman class," which had greater cultural homogeneity, more self-confidence, and more of a tendency to pool its power than a similar class in most other countries. There are closer ties and a more easy understanding between upper class persons in the various professions and businesses in this country than anywhere else. They travel more than in other countries; being together on a Pullman train brings people together intimately. They meet constantly for conferences. They are accustomed to being dynamic and courageous and taking big risks. They know how to cooperate and even how to sacrifice for a common cause. They feel responsibility for the whole nation, as they view its interest, partly because they usually have a long line of American ancestry. The "Pullman class" has been fairly open to talent from below and has contained a disproportionate amount of the nation's brains and courage. Its members have been willing and prepared to take the leadership made so easy for them by the inertia of the masses. . . .

The present observer is inclined to view the American pattern of individual leadership as a great strength of this nation, but the passivity of the masses as a weakness. These two cultural traits of America have, in their historical development, been complementary. But individual activity and mass activity are not necessarily antagonistic principles. It is possible to envisage a future development where the masses in America participate more intensively in political activities of various sorts, but where, nevertheless, outstanding individuals are permitted to have wide space for their initiative according to the great American tradition. Such a social system, if it ever developed, would realize in the highest degree the age-old ideal of a vitalized democracy. It would result not only in a decrease in the immense class differences in America, but more fundamentally, it would effect a higher degree of integration in society of the many millions of anonymous and atomized individuals: strengthening of the ties of loyalty running through the entire social fabric; a more efficient and uncorrupted performance of all public functions; and a more intense and secure feeling on the part of the common citizen of his belongingness to, responsibility for, and participation in the commonwealth as a great cooperative human endeavor—a realization of a fuller life.*

The term "Pullman class" has, of course, been made obsolete by the development of transportation. But generally I tend to believe in the characterization of American political dynamics given in that and some other chapters of that old book of mine.

* *An American Dilemma* (New York, Harper, 1944), pp. 714-716.

PART II

International Implications of Economic Stagnation in America

CHAPTER 8

Frustration

America Is Not a Good Loser

In United States foreign relations a difference in economic growth rate can immediately be translated into a difference in the power to press toward solutions of international problems that satisfy America's interests and ideals. America, of course, still has a higher average output per head than other countries—though for various reasons, which it would take me too long to develop, statistical comparisons with other rich countries, more advanced as welfare states, are apt to exaggerate the difference in output per head, because there are items of collective consumption which become easily underestimated in national accounting and because there are more disutilities and costs in a less perfectly organized society. When the fact that America is dawdling, though not behind but in front of other countries, is accentuated by its present exchange difficulties, this is reflected in a still greater restriction in its freedom to move and act on the international scene.

When as a Swede and an internationalist I am eager that America be strong, it is because I feel that in the main America stands for interests and ideals that I share. This broad consensus does not, of course, prevent my differing on many specific issues from the policy of Washington. This is ordinarily also the position of Americans, to whose inalienable rights it belongs to have their own opinions and to be against the government.

And as America's political system is government through discussion—where, incidentally, more than in any other country foreign voices, even when they are critical, are listened to if they are in tune with basic American ideals—no opportune tactical position in America becomes frozen and remains unchallenged and settled. By trial and through many errors a policy in line with these ideals will continually reassert itself.

As long as America is strong, I need hardly fear that in the longer run views with which I do not sympathize will prevail. The catharsis of free and critical discussion results in a continuous realignment of American policy with its fundamental ideals, which I share. But this process is more effective the more successful America is in organizing its national life along lines of rapid and steady progress and the more powerful it therefore becomes in the world. This means that *what I really fear is American weakness.*

Not only experience but study have made me suspicious about that particular idea in our common Judaeo-Christian heritage that misfortunes and sufferings are generally good for human beings. I have instead increasingly come to believe in health and strength as building not only morale but morals. In any case, as the American's personality has been molded by his rather extraordinary history, he is a brilliant, magnanimous and broad-minded winner, but not a particularly good loser.

While I am perfectly at ease with an America on the way to solving its problem of rapid and steady economic development at home and thus retaining its full voice in the international concert, I shudder to think of all the serious and extremely dangerous mistakes an America, frustrated by a sense of losing out in the economic race, may commit. I am inclined to look upon most of what I consider to be wrong American policies in the international field in recent years as caused by a frustrating feeling of weakness, not the releasing one of strength.

Frustration Has Wider Roots

Now, present international developments are of a nature to cause strong feelings of frustration, even apart from this particular cause. For a basically peace-loving nation with its ambitions directed toward the civilian values of a good life, the revolutionary turmoil in all the poor regions of the world, the difficulty of seeing clearly through what is really happening there and of foreseeing what will come to happen even within the near future, the uncertainty about what can be done to assure the dominance in the world at large of its inherited ideals and, indeed, anxiety about its own security, as all this evolves in the ominous setting of the cold war, is deeply disturbing. The recent relative economic stagnation of the American economy and the realization that America is losing strength and international power, accentuated by its present exchange difficulties, are taking place in a world situation and in a state of mind in America that are already upset by a great number of events inhibiting calm rational thinking about means and ends in terms of basic ideals.

The framework for our study of the international implications of the recent relative economic stagnation in America should therefore rightly need to be a survey of the entire world political situation. This cannot be undertaken in this book. We should be aware, however, that there are many other reasons for a feeling of frustration in America, which must tend to reflect itself in irrational policies. In this situation relative economic stagnation is an aggravating element.

CHAPTER 9

Relations
with the Soviet Block

The United States Policy Towards China

FROM this principle of not attempting to analyze the whole background of United States foreign relations but focusing on relations in which the relative economic stagnation has direct relevance I will make two exceptions: the United States policy toward China and, in particular, its blocking of China's representation in the United Nations, and the policy in regard to licensing strategic exports to the Soviet bloc. I make these exceptions because they illustrate the mechanism of frustration.

In 1949 the Chiang Kai-shek government in China succumbed and the Communists took over the rule of that huge, old and for such a long time severely maltreated empire. This was, of course, a conspicuous failure of earlier American policy. The Truman government acted quite rationally in the beginning. It recognized the failure. It published a comprehensive and honest report on how gross inefficiency, lack of progressive policies to improve the conditions of the masses, and pyramidal wholesale corruption in the previous government and administration had invited this failure, and how the American government had not succeeded in making that government reform itself and its policies.

Great Britain and the Scandinavian countries, which have an old-established diplomatic tradition of recognizing *faits accomplis* and are careful not to emotionalize their foreign policy, established diplomatic relations right away and as a matter of course with the new regime in China. These countries are, of course, highly respected in America and are, together with Switzerland, Holland, the United States, Canada, Australia and New Zealand, the world's most stable democracies of a politically conservative type. They are anything but inclined to favor either revolutions in general or Communism in particular—Communism in Western Europe is powerful and dangerous only elsewhere on the continent. President Truman's Secretary of State, Dean Acheson, let it be known that even if the United States, which has different diplomatic traditions, could not do the same as these otherwise so like-minded countries and, in particular, could not accept the consequence of actively working for China's representation in the United Nations by the government actually in control of the country, it would be prepared to be outvoted in the United Nations General Assembly. So far so good.

There were, indeed, very important reasons for having this done, and done quickly, and the then Secretary General of the United Nations, Trygve Lie, courageously took a well reasoned stand for the change of the representation of China in the United Nations. He did this on the basis of the principle of the universality of the world organization.

Even aside from the rationality of that important principle, there were strong and special reasons in the case of China. We have to remember that this huge empire where nearly a quarter of the people of the world are living—a proportion that is bound to increase—has never had normal relations with foreign countries. During the several thousands of years during which China had been an independent and unified country—under a more or less centralized state—it was in an extraordinary way a boundless country with tremendous mountains, deserts, malaria-infected jungles in all directions and, of course, the ocean to the east. From time to time China stretched out its suzerainty onto the other side of these natural impediments.

It was, indeed, natural that China became highly ethnocentric and looked upon itself as above relations with the outside world founded upon equality of status. The emissaries from foreign countries, when occasionally they came to China, appeared either representing feudal clients or were persons who seemed of no interest from a Chinese point of view. Then came the century-long intrusion of the great powers, pressing for trading facilities and extraterritorial rights for their officials and businessmen, and usually settling their rivalries between themselves and then pressing powerless China to agree. Neither was this what we can call normal foreign relations.

Now China was again sovereign within its own territory. And it found itself excluded from normal political relations with the outside world and, to an extent, from normal trade relations due to the United States' pressure on other countries. With the history I sketched, it is not difficult to understand that the Chinese, even apart from the aggravating factor of their living under Communist rule, should be filled with resentment against the Western world.

The exclusion of China from the United Nations on flimsy legal grounds worked for many years primarily in the interest of the Soviet Union which had every reason to be grateful for the United States' success in isolating China from contacts with the Western countries so that it was thrown entirely into the arms of the Soviet Union. In later years it has become a national goal of China itself as conceived by its Communist rulers. A blind hatred of the United States in particular has become a regular policy technique consolidating the new China. This is more tragic since the United States had been relatively the most decent of the Great Powers that had been oppressing China for a century. As we know, this had resulted in reciprocally friendly feelings between China and the United States which continued up to the events we are now discussing.

Some years after Stalin's death the Polish government conceived the idea of wanting to demonstrate independent initiative by raising at the United Nations in a major way the question of China's representation there. The foreign minister of Poland called in the Chinese ambassador to tell him this decision of his government. To his surprise the Chinese ambassador was not grateful at all but sternly advised the Polish government to abstain from anything besides the usual routine propaganda moves to establish the principle and to induce the American government to go into action in order to put pressure on governments to prolong the exclusion. The conclusion could be drawn that China was now simply not interested in becoming a member of the United Nations and having to defend its various policies before a world audience. I do not believe that this position of China has changed.

And so, as we know, a situation has been prolonged over the years in which China is not participating in the United Nations. From a long-range and global point of view it should, of course, have been essential that that huge country which, as I said, has had no experience of normal international relations during its many thousands of years of existence as a nation-state, should participate in that nursery school for international living—meeting representatives from other countries, having to plead before an audience of them all, sitting in committees, drafting resolutions, lobbying, and so forth. This was in the interest of the whole world even more than that the new and bewildered small countries in Africa and elsewhere should do so. That educational function of the United Nations is a very important one, which we should not forget when we rightly criticize the governments in the United Nations for not permitting it to function more effectively.

When I regret this, and criticize the United States for

having caused it, I happen to express the official view of Sweden, of the other Scandinavian nations and even of Great Britain, though the latter country, having a particular interest in preserving its precarious "special relation" with the United States, would certainly avoid being too outspoken on the issue. I mention that in passing, not stressing it as important to me, since I have no ambition at all to be an official spokesman for anybody, but am entirely satisfied to speak as an independent scholar on the basis of what I believe I know about the facts and of my ideals.

In retelling this sad story, my interest as an observer is to try to understand how the United States came to follow the course of policy which primarily determined the outcome. As I mentioned, in the early months after the Communists succeeded in seizing power in China, the Truman government made its honest and self-critical appraisal of what had happened and prepared itself to accept, and adjust itself to, the representation of China in the United Nations by the government in actual control of the country. However, rather alone among my American and European friends I had grave forebodings.

America, I said to myself and to my friends, has never learned to be a good loser: striking a line after a misfortune, accepting the result of a failure, and then rationally and courageously planning to go ahead again under the changed conditions. We in Europe have all had our great reverses from time to time. We have lost wars; boundaries have been moved. And we have lived on. American wars have regularly begun in a scandalous mess of unpreparedness—even the last war. But after a great national effort they have always ended in complete victory. The whole American experience has been one of ultimate, glorious, and staggering success. This has gone into the soul of the American nation.

Here was America meeting a great failure for the first time in its history. And it was, again for the first time, absolutely irredeemable, at least in the short run. America could not possibly send its army to China in order to strike down the Communist regime. It had to accept the setback as an accomplished fact. Would America be able to do this in a sane and calm mood? Would America even be able to understand how such an extraordinary thing could have happened: that America was defeated? Would not America, instead, turn inwards in self-recrimination and search for traitors in its own government? And would not that frustrate the sensible policy of cutting the losses and marching ahead, inaugurated so wisely and courageously by Truman and Acheson?

Unfortunately, these forebodings were more realistic than anybody could have foreseen. The point I want to stress in the present context is that the American China policy from 1949 on was initially caused by a feeling of frustration on the part of the American people. This happened before and independently of the Korean War. As always, the political situation actually created consolidated itself by inducing events and conditions ensuring its continuation. And so it becomes increasingly difficult to change it, even if it was and remains ill-considered. The main conclusion I want to draw is that frustration is not the ground on which the seeds of enlightened rational thinking and acting can germinate.

As I have mentioned I do not believe that China is now interested in having any change in its relations with the United States and the United Nations.* The international isolation of China can therefore probably not be broken, even if the United States should change its policy. This isolation constitutes one of the most dangerous elements in the present world situation.

* China also knows its weight, and knows that when it really matters—as when the French colonial war in Indochina had to be stopped or when a truce in Laos was desired—forms outside the United Nations have to be found to bring China into negotiations. The same would have to happen, of course, if there were any real progress in the disarmament negotiations.

The Policy of Licensing Strategic Exports

I will take another example of irrational American policy, also originating in the period before the present relative stagnation of the American economy became visible: the strategic export licensing policy in trade with the Soviet countries, which America more or less effectively pressed upon its allies in Western Europe. It had its beginning a little earlier, but it broke out into the open when the United States stopped the delivery of a steel factory to Czechoslovakia in Spring 1948, though it had been ordered, manufactured, and packed in America for shipment and delivery, and had been paid for by the Czechs. At that time I was told by responsible State Department officials that the government was working on normalizing things but that they needed some time to get a number of generals and senators to see sense.

Then came the Berlin blockade and the cause was lost. A tremendous list of things not to be exported to the Soviet countries was put together—at one time including even bathing suits. An interallied agency was set up in Paris where the unwilling allied governments in Western Europe were put under active United States diplomatic pressure to conform. Amendments in Congress were passed, giving teeth to the policy.

I had at that time a very wise and experienced high French official on my staff in the Economic Commission for Europe who in the course of his life had been in on most of the attempts to carry out blockades after the First World War. He wearily reflected that he had learned the hard way that a blockade, to be effective and useful for political purposes, should aim at a small number of commodities and be directed against a limited territory, and only be operated for a short time. Here was a blockade aimed at stopping the export of a very great list of commodities to a very large part of the world and, apparently, for an unlimited time. He threw up his hands and deplored the inability of human beings to think critically and straight and to learn from experience.

For almost a decade I was in the position of following rather closely the effects of this strategic licensing policy and I have even afterwards been interested in seeing what has happened. The effects were almost completely adverse from the point of view of the American policy makers, and this quite aside from the fact that there were leakages in the blockade all the time. To begin with, this policy gave the Soviet countries a propaganda argument that was not entirely lost even in Western Europe where from the beginning the whole policy was looked upon with more than skepticism. Much more important, however, were its effect within the Soviet bloc. It, indeed, greatly helped Stalin and his cadre of politicians throughout the bloc to consolidate his empire.

He could effectively point to this attempted blockade as a proof of the deep animosity of the Western world and, in particular, as showing its determination to do its utmost to hamper economic development in Soviet countries. The comprehensiveness of the list for many years was useful for Stalin and his subordinates in Russia and in all the other countries of the bloc. More specifically they could point out that the countries in the Soviet bloc had to be entirely self-reliant or rely on each other and, in particular, upon the "great Soviet Union" for almost all the things they needed to carry out their development plans.

This propaganda was very effective, and it was essential to Stalin particularly in the beginning, before he had finally purged the governments in Eastern Europe of every trace of their desire for national independence.

Moreover, insofar as the strategic licensing policy had any influence at all on the direction of investments and

production in the Soviet countries, it strengthened the
motives these countries should have had in any case,
namely to make themselves independent of imports of
commodities that were of strategic importance. Planning
in these countries is anything but perfect and anyhow
was not very advanced in the early postwar years. The
secret list, which was certainly not secret to the Soviet
governments, undoubtedly conveyed some useful suggestions about how the Soviet countries should direct their
economic planning.

Against these adverse effects should be counted the
effects of slowing down economic development in the Soviet countries, their armament production and, in particular, their advance in the production of militarily more
effective weapons. Without having the space to give the
reasons for my opinion on this point, I have to restrict
myself to stating the conclusions I have reached from
rather long and intensive observations of what then happened in the Soviet countries. These desired effects of the
strategic licensing policy were very minor, and this was
not merely the result of the leakages which occurred all
the time.

There are similarities between these two illustrations
of unfortunate policies. As in the case of the American
position on China's representation in the United Nations,
the United States government had a more rational attitude in the beginning and tried to resist the demands for
clamping down on Western trade with the Soviet bloc. In
both cases it also met considerable resistance from allied
countries upon which it pressed its policies. In both
cases the American government had had to adjust to a
public opinion dominated by an intense feeling of frustration, bred by the day-to-day manifestations of the Cold
War.

In the latter case we see, however, a gradual move towards a more rational policy. The issue can no longer be
exaggerated in Congress as it was in earlier years. The
list itself is being reduced to what really matters from a

strategic point of view, namely a few products of advanced technology which are of specific importance for armament production. Even neutral Sweden has for a very long time required government licensing for export of arms—which as a matter of routine is quietly handled with much circumspection—and Swedish industry in its own competitive interests is rather careful in not parting with the results of its technological research if it happens to be ahead of other countries. In time not very much more will remain of these export controls which were such a heated issue a short time ago. This will then be the result of a return to common sense. In this process the issue has also lost most of its political and economic advantages for the Soviet bloc.*

These two illustrations have a special importance for the subject of this book. For it must be foreseen that, if America is not soon able to overcome relative economic stagnation, and as it then increasingly experiences the frustration of losing out in the economic race and, as a consequence, loses some power to influence world events, there is a danger that more such mistaken policies will be pressed upon the government, and also that some old and established ones will tend to be perpetuated and perhaps become hardened. I have, as I said, an immense confidence that a strong America, solving its economic problems at home and retaining its full voice in the international concert, will, through trials and many errors, increasingly become wiser and ever more devoted to its inherited ideals. A weak America will not only lose influence but use the influence it has for the wrong pur-

---

* As this is being written, American attempts to stop deliveries to the Soviet Union of steel tubes, contracted for new oil pipelines, are reported in the press. The attempt was turned down in the inter-allied agency in Paris but was pressed in NATO. It resulted only in a recommendation to which, among others, Great Britain took exception. It was a failure, and it caused the Adenauer regime in Western Germany to resort to a very questionable measure in order to stop the parliament in Bonn acting against the United States, compromising again the newly founded democratic rule in the country.

poses and in a wrong way. Because influence is a sort of capital that is spent by using it, there will then be still less of it for rational and purposive use.

The Economic Race with the Soviet Union

The economic race with the Soviet Union has now been brought within the focus of most Americans in a particularly forceful way. The Soviet leaders have challenged America to that race and have defined their economic development goals in terms of raising their production per head to the level of, and thereafter above, the levels of the Western countries and, ultimately, above that even of the United States.

Comparisons of the statistics on output in America and in the Soviet Union have inherent difficulties in that the economic structures are different and basic definitions dissimilar. And there are many possibilities, utilized on both sides, for playing "the numbers game" in such a way that one's own side appears to be winning more rapidly or losing more slowly than the other party is asserting.

For the present purpose it is enough to take it as established that at present the rate of economic growth is considerably higher in the Soviet Union than in the United States, by at least double and perhaps more, and particularly so in the case of heavy industry and of the facilities for education, research, and health protection. Even though the level of the national product in the Soviet Union is still much lower than in the United States, the power of the principle of compound interest implies that, if the United States should not soon succeed in overcoming its relative economic stagnation, the Soviet Union would within a not too distant future approach, reach, and eventually surpass the United States in important fields. If, on the other hand, the United States could substantially raise and also stabilize its rate of growth, Americans could look on Soviet accomplishments with much more equanimity and, perhaps, even with satisfaction and sympathy.

The effect of the one or the other outcome of this race is partly psychological, which does not mean that it is without real significance. Such an effect undoubtedly operates upon the Americans themselves, who are a racing-minded people, as well as upon other nations, not least upon the huge underdeveloped world. It is commonly asserted in America and elsewhere that there is a race on between India and China. The demonstration effect of the outcome of that race should not be underestimated. But the Soviet Union has challenged the United States itself, the richest country in the world. That latter race is immensely more important for the way people in America and the world at large are going to feel and act.

But aside from that psychological effect which has political importance by itself, the growth rate is directly translatable into economic power. If only America could retain its economic strength, I believe economic progress in the Soviet Union should not necessarily be looked upon merely as a danger and a disadvantage. It could be the one thing which ultimately would gradually free it from its strong and obvious feelings of inferiority, suspicion, and aggression, and which would also move it toward greater liberties for its people and a loosening up of its totalitarian and monolithic system of government. Experiences in the post-Stalin era have not entirely baffled these expectations, held for a long time by humanitarians in all countries.

To this, however, must be added the military problem. The underutilization at present of its productive resources makes it advantageous for the United States to keep its military preparedness on a very high level. Indeed, it even makes increased military expenditure a means of raising the level of economic activity or, in any case, a not unwelcome move from the point of view of upholding the business situation in America. That it would be even easier to carry this armament burden if the American economy were operating at full use of its resources is another thing.

The Soviet Union is in a totally different situation. There increased military expenditures—and successful efforts in conquering the space far outside the earth's stratosphere—are a real sacrifice. Agriculture, in particular, where planning has failed rather dismally from the beginning and continuously to this day, is now becoming an area of real danger. Agriculture is still starved for fertilizers and tractors, and it is officially recognized that the huge and again rising armament expenditures for the time being block the road for producing those things that might overcome that bottleneck. But the sacrifice of agricultural progress and of higher consumption levels is made without hesitation. With rapidly increasing production this situation will change; the strains will be lessened. It is not very encouraging to contemplate that even greater military expenditures will then be possible in the Soviet Union with relatively less real sacrifice.

Towards the end of the war and in the period immediately following the war I did not share the overoptimistic views held in this country of the possibility for close and amiable co-operation between the United States and the Soviet Union in policing the world. At the bottom of the file on me in the State Department there is, as I know, a whole stack of documents showing me as rather undesirably "anti-Russian"—as viewed from the angle that was then somewhat prevalent in Washington.* I was just

---

* During a visit to Washington in the late Fall of 1943 I had some rather strange experiences.

"Once I gave a lecture to a random American audience of civil servants, university professors, and other people interested in public affairs, sponsored by highly placed public figures from both political parties; the lecture was about Scandinavia and the war. In my lecture I was not devoting much interest to the Soviet Union; the views on conditions in the Soviet Union which could perhaps have been inferred from my lecture were the views most Swedes

a typical Swede, under the influence, as we Swedes are, of having had the Russians as close neighbors for a thousand years, and I have, of course, not changed a bit. But many Americans have changed considerably not from being Communist sympathizers, which exceedingly few were, but from having naive hopes about postwar collaboration with Soviet Russia.

---

had and have and, in the main, the same as I hold today after considerably more study and experience. Even while I was speaking I felt uncomfortably that the audience was critical and unfriendly to an extent I was not accustomed to in America. After the lecture there was an outburst of what I regarded as rather naive questions implying that I had been unappreciative of the Soviet Union, by not talking more about that country and not taking up a number of things. Didn't I know that there was religious freedom in the Soviet Union? Why hadn't I mentioned that the Soviet Union had the most democratic constitution in the world? Wasn't it worth while pointing out that 'in a deeper sense' the trade unions in the Soviet Union were more democratic than the A.F. of L. and the CIO? Why had I not understood the significance of the fact that, after the end of the war, the United States and the Soviet Union were going to collaborate in settling all world problems, including those in the Scandinavian corner which I had talked about? I had apparently not understood that the United States relied upon the Soviet Union to exert a great influence on the problems I had been discussing.

"At another occasion about the same time I participated in a meeting of distinguished experts on foreign affairs from the administration and the universities. Among many other things that were new and strange to me, I was then informed that American thinking was developing on the lines that only the Great Powers should be allowed to have any military defense forces, while small countries like my own would be disarmed in the interest of world peace. I recall that the former Swedish Minister to Washington, Mr. Waldemar Boström, who was with me on that occasion, took very firmly the same position I did, which perhaps it is unnecessary now to elaborate.

"A Swede is apt to remember also one practical effect of this turn of mind—the emphatic refusal of the United States to do anything to influence their great ally to give Finland easier peace terms; Britain took the same line. It was left to the Swedes alone, as the Finns' only friend in court, to do their best to get a reasonable peace settlement with the Soviet Union—and particularly to strive for a scaling down of the war indemnities—and to help them economically during a most difficult period. Immediately after the end of the war in Europe, however, the Finns could not merit any credits or other considerations from the United States

Even if I was not taken in as so many, though by far not all, American liberal intellectuals then were—and many more Americans who were neither very liberal nor very intellectual—by pious hopes about the Soviet Union, and even if I foresaw the Cold War,* I never believed that the Soviet Union was likely to try to overcome Western

---

—now, because they were paying war indemnities to the Soviet Union."

The quotation is from footnote 5 to Chapter XIV of *An International Economy* (New York, Harper, 1956). In the same book I have three sections on the impact of the Cold War, on what I called an emotional cycle in America, and on the effects of it in the social sciences (pp. 302-308). In particular, I was early feeling the danger of uninformed and uncritical views about the Soviet Union among my liberal friends in America and foresaw how this would later give them an interest in demonstrating an equally irrational contrary bias in their thinking on world issues, implying a dilution of inherited liberal ideals. (*Ibid*, pp. 304 ff.) Already in 1944 I had written:

"The admiration for the Soviet Union tends generally to bring Americans to the attitude that ends justify the means and that might takes precedence over right. This tendency, even if yet not so strong, towards a dilution of the Americans' liberal idealism might turn out to be one of the most important and most fateful of the developments we are now witnessing" (*Warnung für Friedensoptimismus* [Zürich, Europa Verlag, 1945], p. 39, translation from the Swedish original published in January 1944).

In 1956, during the McCarthy era, I added in the same spirit:

"I am convinced that several of the roots of the present weakness of liberalism in America—which in its entire history has been the great and, as a trend, the dominant moral force—go back to confused thinking and opportunistic choosing and manipulation of facts during this period at the end of the Second World War" (*An International Economy*, p. 306).

And, more specifically:

"Undoubtedly . . . during the downward phase of the emotional cycle in the cold war and because of the memory of their own attitudes a few years ago (and almost in self-defense and self-justification when pleading to their own conscience) they have often felt compelling reasons to out-Herod Herod in the popular revulsion against Soviet ideology and policy. Quite apart from any pressure of McCarthyism and other forms of crude retroactive thought control, it is easily understandable if, after their emotional history of the last fifteen years, the liberals have become a little dazed and uncertain. To a considerable extent they share this experience with the rest of their nation." (*Ibid*, p. 305.)

* *Warnung Vor Friedensoptimismus*, pp. 197 ff. *et passim;* more elaborated in the Swedish original, 1944.

Europe by military conquest. Such a policy would be strongly against all Russian traditions, as we Swedes have learned to know them through long and intensive experience, and also against their faith in the economic superiority of their economic system, which we all know about. On this point, too, I am inclined to keep to my earlier opinions. This view is optimistic if at the same time I can believe that we can keep up a progressive economy not only in Western Europe but also in America. This view would, of course, be less optimistic if America should not raise and stabilize its rate of economic growth.

I would even believe that a substantially higher rate of economic growth in the United States would make the Soviet leaders more inclined to enter upon a course of seeking agreements on various points to lessen tension in the world and, in particular, make them prepared earnestly to seek agreement on a beginning of disarmament. A continuation of the present relative stagnation in America, on the other hand, might tempt them to follow a different course, particularly as such a development in America is apt to keep the Western countries split, as I will touch upon in the next chapter.

I am then assuming that America really wants a lessening of tension and a development towards gradually liquidating the present precarious armament race. That Americans are basically a peace-loving nation is one of my strongly held views, founded upon direct observation since my early youth. But I cannot close my eyes to the fact that even the present low rate of economic growth in America is preserved only by extraordinarily large and rising armaments expenditures. This is not a healthy situation for a nation that, I am convinced, is honestly trying to reach an end to the armament race.

On an abstract level economists can argue that a major decrease of these expenditures can easily be compensated. I have myself taken part in one of the conferences of economists holding out this prospect. But we should be aware of the real difficulties implied if there is not a radical change in the way the American people and the Congress look upon the role of government in the American economy. The difficulties of an adjustment of the American economy to substantially lower levels of armament expenditures are greater because the growth rate is so low. In a rapidly growing economy a decrease in armament expenditures could be taken more in stride.

Nor should we hide from ourselves the fact that the tremendous size of the military establishment, with the huge armament industry behind it, means there are powerful vested interests in keeping up those expenditures. President Eisenhower had a pertinent remark on this point in his last public address to the American public as President: ". . . in the councils of government, we must guard against the acquisition of unwarranted influence, whether sought or unsought, by the military-industrial complex."

These vested interests, working against an international agreement to decrease armaments substantially, must have much more appeal and be politically much more forceful in an economy with high and rising unemployment and underutilized capacity.

CHAPTER 10

Relations
with Western Europe

The Marshall Plan

THE importance of keeping up America's economic strength in its relations with the Soviet world is obvious and does not need to be elaborated further. America's willingness to assist and aid the underdeveloped countries and its ability to exert a wholesome leadership among the other rich countries on this problem are also seriously hampered by a low growth rate at home and acute difficulties in meeting additional demands for foreign exchange. I will revert to this latter question below.

There has been little open discussion about America's need to be economically strong in its ordinary relations with its friends and allies among the rich countries, particularly in Western Europe. In recent years the American President must often have felt tempted to sigh: "God save me from my friends; my enemies I can take care of myself."

I happened to observe at close range America's great rescue action in Western Europe during the latter part of the forties and the beginning of the fifties. In that Marshall Plan period the United States by a magnificent policy move reversed its rather niggardly and unenlightened attitude to the international exchange problem that was reflected in the Bretton Woods agreement as it emerged after the inner fighting and final collusion between Lord Keynes and Harry White.

Indeed, the United States did all it could to transfer favors to Western Europe in order to make the countries in that subregion strong enough to stand on their own feet economically. In doing this, it took the utmost care to hold back and not to use its power. It advised the European governments to make up their own minds, promising to support any constructive policy they could agree upon among themselves financially and in other ways.

America then had a very clear conception of what should have been done in Europe. Towards the end of that period I wrote that American businessmen, administrators and economists who took a leading part in the rescue mission were among the very best Europeans. But in that period of the great dollar shortage, *when America had all the power, it largely abstained from using it.* I should confess that at that time I often wished that the American government, though keeping in the main to its line of merely helping Western Europe to help itself, would nevertheless have actively pressed the Europeans a little more to follow American intentions for their aid, which in the main I thought then, as I do now, to be in the common interest of Europe and the world. Exceptions were due only to some outbreaks of frustration when, on the contrary, America really pressed its European clients to the utmost, as exemplified by the strategic export licensing policy touched upon in the previous chapter.

The United States permitted the West European countries to discriminate bluntly against its exports without raising any complaints. This was part of the great design, and the United States actually assisted in planning the West European commercial and financial discriminatory policies against itself. In the Economic Commission for Europe, which was my point of observation, the United States actively supported Poland and other European coal-producing countries in their efforts to make Europe self-sufficient in coal. Its representatives argued that it was unnatural to ship coal over the ocean. This policy was carried out against the opposition of the coal industry in America and of the big ports which were doing their best to press the United States government to reverse this policy in their interests. It also happened in this early Marshall Plan period, to take another example, that the United States government took initiatives to stop American oil monopolies from carrying on an exploitative price policy in Western Europe.

The main dish served to the West Europeans in this postwar period was, of course, the tremendous financial aid, amounting to almost $30 billion of which two thirds were straight grants—not reckoning the military aid. This was many times the original dollar input in the International Monetary Fund and the International Bank of Reconstruction and Development.

Overgenerosity

I felt at that time that all the financial aid should have been given in the form of loans on easy terms to be repaid when the West European countries had regained their economic viability, and I held that view in spite of the fact, which I should not now conceal, that I then underestimated the rapidity by which that goal could be reached. It would still have been "aid," since there was at that time no basis for loans to Western Europe on commercial banking terms.

The overgenerous terms applied by the United States are easily explainable. The West European countries who had been in the war were seriously damaged and standards of living were down. America, on the other hand, had had the experience, rather unique in world history, of its people enjoying rising living levels both during the war and afterwards. It had entered the war in a state of depression and unemployment, and the war accomplished what the New Deal failed to do, rapidly raising employment. A "sharing of wealth" seemed a natural course to both Americans and Europeans.

Nevertheless, I feel that I was right in my judgment at that time. It was sharing only between the rich. The whole international exchange situation would have been different and much more wholesome today if America in the last five years could have called in payment from the West European governments for financial aid given them in the Marshall period—gradually and with due consideration of their exchange position. America's record makes it certain that such considerations would have been taken in a spirit of generosity and friendliness.

I find it difficult to understand why this reflection is never made in American discussions about the present international exchange situation, even if it is perhaps understandable that it is never pointed to in Western Europe. The blunt fact is that countries such as Germany, France, and now Italy, that had a few years ago received billions of dollars as gifts from the United States, have now reached a capacity to produce and export that makes it possible for them to stack up the excessive gold holdings and liquid dollar assets which are the real core of present exchange difficulties for the United States.

I never believed that *giving aid as gifts from one government to another is a natural, a necessary, or even a wise policy—except when the beneficiary is an underdeveloped country that has deep-seated and structural disabilities to overcome.* Neither do such gifts create much gratitude or form a firm basis for friendship. It is, of course, a fact—and I pointed it out at that time, too—that the two countries in Europe without a trace of anti-Americanism in the postwar era, and which have none today, are Sweden and Switzerland.

Their economies were less in disarray, since they had not only tried, as most countries did, but had succeeded in staying out of the war. Psychologically they had not acquired the *pauvres honteux* mentality of the rest of the subregion—though in this connection we should not forget either that much poorer Finland, through all its misfortunes, ever since the end of the First World War and even during the Second World War had proudly kept as a basic principle for its national financial policy that it wants to pay back whatever it gets from abroad.

In the Marshall Plan period it was natural, not only for Switzerland, who did not need any financial assistance, but also for Sweden to decline to take grants. The Swedes insisted on having the financial aid they, too, at that time needed in the form of loans that should be paid back. They did so sometimes actually against kind proddings from American officials that they should take some grants like all the others in the interest of "equality" and "co-operation," a degree of generosity on the part of the United States which they found exaggerated.* As I will later point out, these two countries have also insisted on paying for their armament expenditures themselves.

The United States relationship with Western Europe is now on an entirely different basis from what it was in the Marshall Plan period. America is well entitled to feel satisfied that its rescue action was so successful that most European countries now enjoy a rapid and steady growth. But the United States in its present exchange difficulties should have reason to regret that it had been unnecessarily overgenerous.

In planning the rescue action in Western Europe the banking and financial experts were not given much say. I do not mean that they should have been permitted to decide upon a political issue, such as that of what help Western Europe urgently needed. But particularly in regard to forms and modalities they have certain traditions, founded upon experiences and knowledge, that should not have been thrown away lightheartedly.†

* At a later stage the Swedes actually accepted also some grants of which they should not be very proud.

† It is true that America's experiences in international finance up till the Second World War had been slight and mostly unfortu-

Changed Power Relations

But what was done cannot now be remedied so why cry over spilled milk? I only insist on stressing it in this context because it has decisively contributed to the different power relations between the United States and its allies in Western Europe as of today, compared with what this relation was in the early years after the war under the scepter of the great dollar shortage, and with what it could have been with a more prudent policy on the part of the United States.

Surprisingly enough, bulging economic and financial strength has in a particular degree descended upon the countries in Western Europe which had been most harassed by the war and therefore relatively most weakened,

---

nate. I could at that time not help feeling a certain nostalgia for private international finance that certainly had its code of prudent behavior seriously damaged by the overgenerous American way of helping Europe and its later reflection on the decision of how to meet the very different assistance needs of the rest of the world.

"America, with its unstable traditions and sad experiences in international finance, and faced with the necessity of giving funds outright to governments, has involuntarily contributed to killing the idea of international finance as a business proposition by insisting on calling all its reconstruction loans after the war aid or assistance.

"The distinction between aid and credit should have been clearly made and continuously stressed. By insisting instead on systematically throwing everything into the mixed pot of 'aid' and 'assistance,' the Americans have—certainly without intending to do so —inflicted an injury on the socially useful assumption that international finance is business. There is no doubt that a less sentimental and more selfish people would have handled a similar situation differently—with less generosity, probably, but with more respect for established business mores." (*An International Economy* [New York, Harper, 1956], pp. 115-114; see also pp. 111, 112 *et passim.*)

namely defeated Germany and Italy together with those countries that had been overrun by the Nazis and were later liberated by the Great Alliance of the United States, the Soviet Union, and Great Britain. This is pretty much "das neue Europa" or "die Festung Europa" of Hitler's dreamworld, except that it has lost some of the Eastern dependencies which have disappeared behind the Iron Curtain.

All these Western countries on the European continent are still weak in many and very fundamental respects. They have serious unsettled psychological and moral problems to cope with.* Except for quasi-Scandinavian Holland, democracy is in them as yet only a rather frail tendril. France is ruled by popular referenda in a Bonapartean manner, perfected by the monopolistic use of the modern instruments of mass communication, especially television, while parliament is mutilated and moribund, and the people politically split and apathetic. But economically these countries are striding ahead rapidly though from comparatively low levels, particularly of workers' wages. This rapid economic progress had begun long before they consolidated themselves into a protective custom union.

The snag is that meanwhile the United States has lapsed into relative economic stagnation and that internationally its economic weakness has become accentuated by exchange difficulties. At present the United States has good reasons to urge fundamental changes in the policies of its European allies in many and diverse fields. But it no longer has the economic strength to press for them very effectively. The United States even has to present its demands *sotto voce,* or has to adjust them to very strange doctrines adhered to in the increasingly powerful and self-conscious bloc on the European continent.

* These psychological and moral problems are more specifically set out in Tord Ekström, Gunnar Myrdal, and Roland Pålsson, *Vi och Västeuropa* (Stockholm, 1962), pp. 29 ff., 40 ff.

The situation could not be more of a reversal from what it was ten or fifteen years ago. Then the United States had all the power but used it mostly with utmost caution and, I would say, unselfishness—though as usual its spokesmen in a mood of perverted Puritanism tried their best to convince the nation and others that it acted "solely in the interest of the United States," a confession that was eagerly grasped on the continent of Europe and sometimes even in England* as a reason why no repayment, even in gratitude, was really called for. Now the United States has demands to raise but lacks the strength to back them up.

To state it bluntly, the United States is in danger of losing out as the uncontested leader within the Western world. The danger will increase if the difference in economic growth rates remains. This I regret. In any case it must be adverse to the pursuance of American ideals and interests.

The Defense Burden

During the era of overwhelming United States economic strength it seemed natural to everybody, both in America and Europe, that the United States should carry a major part of the burden for the defense of Western Europe. From the very beginning the countries on the European continent showed little willingness to fulfill even the modest targets for their own contribution to their defense which had, from time to time, been negotiated. Many years ago a Turkish foreign minister wryly confided to me his reflection that on the European conti-

---

* I remember a member of the British Labour Government explaining that the United States badly needed, and for the foreseeable future would continue to need, to give away a large part of its exports in order to prevent depression at home.

nent, outside the Soviet bloc, there were only three effective military machines, and all three—the Yugoslav, the
Swedish and the Swiss—were outside NATO. Britain, of
course, continued to carry a heavy defense burden and,
like the United States, continued to keep much of its
forces on the continent. Recently the rearmament of
Western Germany represents a big change. But otherwise
the situation remains largely as it was.

Meanwhile, the United States for years also had to
carry the moral and political burden of first the Dutch
and then for a much longer period the French utilizing
American weapons or, anyhow, weapons their countries
could at that time not have afforded except for the large-
scale American financial aid they had received, for cruel
colonial wars which from the beginning were foredoomed
to total defeat.

In recent years, this situation has now and then been
enlivened by suggestions from France that it would be
better if the United States withdrew its troops from Europe or, more often, that the United States could not be
relied upon to keep them there for long nor to use its
nuclear striking force to defend Western Europe. This
last view is increasingly heard in countries other than
France. These suggestions are usually propounded as a
motivation for the idea that Western Europe or individual
countries there should have their independent nuclear
deterrent.

This idea is not very realistic, calculating the costs involved if the deterrent would have any importance. It
often transpires that its significance would be to guarantee that a world war would really break out, involving
even the United States, if one or several of the Western
countries on the continent of Europe got into conflict with
the Soviet Union. The paradoxical situation is that all
this scheming for an independent little atomic arsenal in
France or other countries in Western Europe is founded
upon the assumption that, if there should be a show-
down, it is nevertheless America's atomic striking power

which is the real deterrent and the real defense of Western Europe.

Meanwhile the United States government, which is not in a strong position for the reasons referred to, has to put a good face on a bad business. It is presenting one proposal after another on a "multinational" atomic force—independent, though dependent, European and at the same time Atlantic—one more curious than the other. These proposals have not met with any enthusiasm either in Europe or the United States itself.

It should not be surprising that this situation in NATO should look particularly upside down to a Swede who thinks back on the brief but crowded postwar history of American relations with its allies on the European continent. Sweden built up a national defense which placed not only a relatively greater financial burden on its budget but was militarily considerably stronger than that of NATO member countries on the European continent. If I am not wrongly informed, Sweden with 7½ million inhabitants still has the fourth-biggest air force in the world—after the United States, the Soviet Union, and Great Britain. Western Germany is now coming up to the same level while France is still behind.

Sweden feels that thereby, and by its general policy in the field of foreign relations, it has created an area of stability in the northern part of Western Europe. It has also abstained from having its own nuclear force though its level of technology would make this a feasible ambition. It has done so mainly in the interest of not contributing to the spread of nuclear weapons. As I said, Sweden and Switzerland are singular in Europe for not being the breeding ground of even the slightest trace of anti-American feelings, nor of nurturing any wishful dreams of wanting to participate in forming a third world power, strong enough to stand up even against the United States.

United States worries about keeping NATO a united and effective alliance, of co-ordinating and directing the defense efforts to maximum over-all usefulness, and of having the financial burden distributed in a reasonably just way do not fall within the range of problems on which I can claim expert knowledge. The only inference which is important in the present context is simply that in dealing with these problems, the United States is now in a much weaker position because it cannot back its military and political arguments with economic strength.

The Burden of Aid to Underdeveloped Countries

I am much more familiar with the problems of a more equitable distribution among the rich countries of the financial burden of "aid" to the underdeveloped countries. Astonishingly enough, until rather recently people in the United States seldom raised this problem, at least not on the scholarly level. I believe I was one of the very first to do it in America in a paper prepared for Columbia University's Bicentennial in May 1954, when I stressed that there was no justification for the United States to shoulder such a disproportionately large part of the burden.* I returned a few years later to this theme in an address at the New School of Social Research from which I will permit myself to quote a few paragraphs because they express the views I still hold. The large-scale financial aid to the countries in Western Europe which had such wholesome effects in making it possible for those countries to regain economic viability and launch rapid economic progress also had, I felt, a detrimental moral effect:

* *An International Economy* (New York, Harper, 1956), pp. 128 ff.

This was that the peoples and the politicians, both in the United States itself and in Western Europe, became conditioned to accept as a normal and right thing that the United States should take upon itself practically the whole of the financial burden of providing international aid in any part of the world where it was required, with purely token contributions coming from other economically advanced nations . . .

A very important moral element of every scheme for distributing income, national as well as international, should be that the burden be shared in a just and equitable manner. It is not fair and will never be felt to be fair that a man who lives in Stockholm, Geneva, or Brussels does not share equally the burden of aid to underdeveloped countries with a man in the same income bracket living in Columbus, Ohio, in Detroit, Michigan, or in Denver, Colorado.

I am inclined to believe that most of the things which are imperfect and wrong in our present aid schemes spring from this lack of justice in their financing.

And I went on to exemplify the last sentence:

When international aid becomes unilateral and politics thus enters into its distribution, both moral and economic standards are apt to crumble. A selection according to political interests is often bound to imply the diversion of aid to the less needy countries or to those least capable of using it effectively for economic advancement.

In the receiving countries, unilateral aid may have equally unfortunate effects. The political conditions of the aid are resented by their peoples. Indeed, political strings and the existence of ulterior motives will be suspected, even when they are not present.

The direction and control of the use of aid will

also in many cases be less efficient. An underdeveloped country may be willing and even grateful to
take from an international agency the advice which
it is not happy or, because of popular resentment,
not able to accept under prodding by a single country, least of all when that country is very rich, powerful and carefree in its public expressions.

This is, of course, one important reason why aid
is best channeled through an international agency.
But it would be almost preposterous to suggest that
more than a minor—indeed, almost only a symbolic
—part of the total flow of aid should be so handled
as long as one country pays almost all of the costs.
A fairer distribution of the financial burden is, therefore, a condition for transferring, on a large scale,
aid and technical assistance to underdeveloped countries into an institutional framework which is multilateral and truly international.

I have suggested in another connection that the
inimical effects of unilateral aid given mainly by
the United States are so serious that—even giving
full consideration to the urgent needs of the underdeveloped countries—I would rather see a short-term
decrease in America's willingness to give international aid than the establishment of the present
pattern as a firm and lasting one. Indeed, the continuation of present conditions will almost inevita-
bly result in a cutting down of American aid.*

What I said then corresponded, I am sure, to what any
ordinary American must have felt on this question. The
awkward thing is that when in recent years the United
States really needed a fairer distribution, since it was
then short of liquid foreign exchange resources, its failing economic strength made it more difficult for the
United States to impress upon the other rich countries

* "Trade and Aid," *The American Scholar,* Vol. 26, No. 2
(Spring 1957), pp. 140-142.

their duty to spend more on aid to underdeveloped countries. There were several occasions when American officials almost went begging to the West European leaders, asking that they consider bigger contributions. This was not the posture that was reasonable for a country that up to 1958, the year when the balance of payments deficit first assumed serious proportions, had spent more than $60 million on grants and foreign aid, of which well over half had gone to the countries of Western Europe, now increasingly prosperous and no longer lacking adequate reserves of their own.

The situation since then has improved considerably though it is still not satisfactory. More decisive than American prodding in bringing about the change have been the West European countries' political and export interests, and also the rise in all rich countries of a popular demand that more should be done for the underdeveloped countries. With these mixed motives it is understandable that much confusion has been preserved by using the term "aid" to cover everything between the extremes of straight gifts for free use on the one hand, to short-term credits on the other, sometimes given at high interest rates, tied to specific exports which are occasionally overpriced at the expense of the underdeveloped countries dependent on receiving even these credits and thus easily exploited. Occasionally even more questionable items are reckoned as aid. It is such throwing very different things together in one bag which makes the term foggy and misleading.

America had originally inaugurated this confusion in the rescue action to Western Europe in the Marshall Plan era.* Now it is retained by a conspiracy of all parties concerned. The poor countries are so dependent on capital inflow that they cannot afford to make an issue of terminology. And the rich countries have an interest in presenting as much as possible of their relations to poor

* See above in footnote, pp. 131-132.

countries as "aid," even that which is profitable business pure and simple, sometimes very profitable. The United States has, in fact, turned out to be the country which is relatively most honest in presenting its accounts with the underdeveloped countries.

Meanwhile not only the total capital flow to underdeveloped countries but also the American part of it have been held far below the magnitude that from time to time is announced as necessary by experts in the field. The pattern of confining the much greater part of "aid" to national and bilateral, instead of international and multilateral, programs has been consolidated, and also that of tying aid to exports from the particular country which gives the "aid."

At the same time students of the development problems of underdeveloped countries are gradually finding out that those problems are much more serious than was believed, that a much bigger capital flow is necessary in order to prevent real calamities in various parts of the world, and that little of that capital can ever be expected to be paid back—on this last and some other related points I cannot agree with the recent Clay report which otherwise has some good points. Overshadowing everything else is the fact that in addition to, and as a basis for, a much increased capital flow to underdeveloped countries, what is really needed is a radical change on the part of the rich countries in their way of doing business with the underdeveloped countries. To the last point I will come back later.

In this serious situation the economic and financial weakness of the United States is, of course, most unfortunate. Today more than ever the world needs strong American leadership in the field of aid to underdeveloped countries. After the experiences which the United States has had and finally digested, it should not be expected simply to raise its own contributions substantially without also insisting that other rich countries do the same. Having maintained economic strength, it could more effectively urge such a course and at the same time think through in more constructive terms the whole issue of rich countries' economic relations to the surrounding world slum.

European Integration

The view that the countries in Western Europe should be economically and, if possible, politically integrated belonged to the American aims for Western Europe in the rescue action under the Marshall Plan. Behind this attitude there were a number of mixed motives. The United States had twice been drawn into world wars that had originated in Europe. A closer integration in Western Europe was later also seen as strengthening the basis for the military alliance the United States had created in NATO. On a more ideological level, a federation of Western Europe was looked upon as natural and desirable by the Americans who were proud of their own union, which had successfully amalgamated people from very diverse origins into one nation.

That last analogy is, however, somewhat confusing for several reasons. In America there was a basis of British tradition which permitted the United States not only to have one language, English, but also to become the world's earliest modern democracy. The country was also new in a sense and rapidly expanding geographically into what was empty but productive land as the western frontier bulged out towards the Pacific Ocean. Even more important, the United States was operating in a political power vacuum limited only by nature.

Western Europe is already fully inhabited, divided into nation-states with distinguished personalities and usually with their own languages. Even aside from the internal rivalries between the several countries in this subregion, the collectivity does certainly not exist in a power vacuum as the United States did when it grew. And the traditions of the countries on the continent are not the British ones. In particular there is little on the European continent of what so early made the United States a firmly anchored democracy. The nations in Western Euorpe that are really similar to the United States in civic ethos, namely Great Britain and the Scandinavian countries, are, and have always been, seafaring and outwardly oriented in their economic as in all their other interests.

To this should be added that the Americans and the European enthusiasts for integration ordinarily tend to exaggerate the importance of the size of the home market for economic progress. There are many economic studies establishing that this popular view is false. The larger countries in Western Europe having around 50 million people each are certainly big enough to realize all opportunities of scale, particularly if they do not turn inwards but are prepared to exert themselves to have foreign markets. Even small but decidedly outward-oriented countries like Sweden have large markets for their chief export commodities.

There are other factors quite distinct from the big home market which are responsible for America's high rate of secular economic growth—high in terms of prewar standards. They have to do with the spirit and the institutions of the country, the richness of its natural resources, and its political stability. We find that a small country like Sweden, well endowed in these respects in the same way as the United States, shows a growth rate per head over a century almost exactly like that of the United States.

From the beginning the discussion of economic integration in Europe was related in a rather confused way to the issue of freer trade. What was first needed was to overcome all the quantitative restrictions which were inherited from the first strenuous years after the war and to restore multilateralism in trade and more freedom in payment relations. Carrying out these aims through negotiations within the O.E.E.C. and the European Payments Union was one of the more solid achievements in West European economic co-operation in the Marshall Plan period. An American contribution to these earlier strivings was its acquiescence in a common discrimination against the United States, which later could largely be dropped as the dollar shortage receded and the chief West European currencies became hard.

The idea of a common wall of discrimination around a more integrated Western Europe remained, however, as a legacy from the earlier period, and this legacy has undoubtedly contributed much to the protectionist spirit of the Common Market that was established later. This spirit of trade discrimination towards the outside world had a sort of ideological sanction in the odd partiality for a customs union, *i.e.* a complete preference system, that was predominant in American thinking, which, on the other hand, had always been adamantly against an incomplete preference system of the type Great Britain had built up in the Commonwealth.

Meanwhile, a most important ideological development had proceeded along quite another line in the United States. That line runs from the devoted labor of Mr. Cordell Hull, President Franklin Roosevelt's liberal-minded Secretary of State, and his collaborators towards the end of the war in preparing for the International Trade Organisation, to the astonishingly rapid acceptance without many distorting amendments of President Kennedy's Trade Expansion Act of 1962 which gives the President power to negotiate a very radical lowering, and partly even complete abolition, of customs barriers.

The line was not straight, as a historical development usually never is. Thus the International Trade Organisation was killed a-borning by the American Congress after all the work had been done to get international acceptance of this American initiative. On the other hand, the

negotiations in G.A.T.T. had already resulted in a considerable lowering of the highly protectionist American
tariffs inherited from the Hawley-Smoot Act. And the
United States had, on the whole, for its own part conservatively adhered to the most-favored-nation clause
which remains a main hope for the striving toward freer
world trade and the prevention of the rise of trading
blocs. The new authority conferred on the President to
negotiate very large tariffs cuts was in many ways a final
step, decisively putting the United States in the free trad-
ers' camp.

At the same time, the United States has demonstrated
a growing awareness that the underdeveloped countries
cannot for their own part join in a general movement to
freer trade. In order to engender development they need
protection of their slender industrial beginnings. The
United States is even becoming gradually prepared to see
and accept the much more radical idea that the rational
thing would indeed be to afford the underdeveloped countries not only an equal but a preferential treatment in the
markets of the rich countries. Such a policy would help
them in their development efforts much more than any
"aid," and it would steer higher export earnings right into
the economies of the underdeveloped countries and not,
as "aid" usually does, through government offices.

This ideological development towards free trade for the
rich countries, while permitting the poor countries to protect themselves and even giving them some preferential
advantages, is not by any means consummated in the
United States. But the direction of the trend of thinking
is unmistakable. That this trend is in line with American
ideals of liberty and equality on a world scale is apparent.

The Common Market and the Collapse of the Brussels Negotiations

THE FIRST ACT

In Western Europe work on economic integration did not start in earnest until the end of the Marshall Plan period and coincided with the development that soon followed when the dollar shortage turned into surpluses. It had its harbinger in the Coal and Steel Community, which in the end came to include only "Little Europe," *i.e.* the six countries that later in 1957 concluded the Rome Treaty and in the following year formed the European Economic Community, in Anglo-Saxon countries mostly known under the euphemistic name of the Common Market.

The timing of the main negotiations implied that the strivings for economic integration were becoming more exclusively a West European affair, though the United States became involved in a way to which I will return shortly. To this must be added the change that then had occurred with the flow of American aid coming to an end and, a little later, the slowing down of the economic growth in the United States and its entrance into a period of exchange difficulties.

From the very beginning of these negotiations as, indeed, already during the earlier negotiations leading to the Coal and Steel Community, there appeared a difference between two groups of countries in Western Europe each with different ideals and ambitions for the future. On the one hand, there were the six continental countries. In various degrees they wanted a tightly knit group of states, held together to some extent by common economic policies but above all by a common tariff against the whole outside world—except for former colonies, mainly the former French colonies in Africa, which would form a small system of satellites. On the other hand, there were Great Britain and the Scandinavian countries joined by Switzerland and Austria—and Portugal. They were primarily interested only in freeing trade in industrial goods in Western Europe, while permitting the participating countries to preserve their individual tariffs as well as—in Britain's case—some preferential treatment and close relations with the Commonwealth.

The latter group of countries were not interested in subjugating themselves to the supranational, bureaucratic system of the Court, the Council and the Executive Commission, which the former group held necessary in order to integrate their economies. This apparatus, operating outside normal parliamentary controls, would have powers above their own constitutions and national laws which they would not think of giving to similar agencies within their own countries.

This group of countries that did not join the Common Market instead put their trust in simply freeing commerce, and were inclined to rely upon the market forces to take care of a mutual adjustment without interference by supranational authorities. Generally they are more outwardly oriented. Specifically they have by and large put fewer hindrance in the way of imports from underdeveloped countries. In recognizing their differences in these and other respects with the former countries, they would have been prepared to let them to join them as a consolidated group in a West European free trade area. When this suggestion was declined even before it was made a definite proposal, the result was the formation of the European Free Trade Association, commonly referred to as E.F.T.A., which started its activities in 1960.

This was the first act in the drama. The two organizations went ahead lowering the internal trade barriers in each of them. I felt critical towards the management of

E.F.T.A. in those years on one point. With the outwardly oriented spirit of the countries in that group they should not have become so fixed in viewing E.F.T.A. as only a counterpart of the Common Market, built up merely to strengthen their bargaining power with Little Europe. They should have turned to the world at large. With their predominant interest in freer trade and the consequent absence of the heavily bureaucratic, supranational apparatus of the Brussels organization, they could have approached the rich countries in Australasia and the poor ones in the rest of the British Commonwealth as well as in Latin America. They could also have approached the United States if it had not bound itself differently in the unfortunate manner I will comment upon below.

In their type of organization they could more easily have accommodated the special interest in permitting the exceptions that most of these non-European countries need and must need. They could, for instance, have permitted the Latin American countries to have their own protective common market, which they need much more badly than the rich Western countries and to which such an offer was suggested. They could perhaps even have helped them to make such an organization effective. The Austrians and Swedes actually did give some suggestions in that direction but met no interest on the part of the Tory government in Britain which was now preparing to reverse its stand by applying for membership in the Common Market.

THE SECOND ACT WITH THE FINALE

The British government took this move in the Summer of 1961. It did it unilaterally, without asking the other governments in E.F.T.A. and in the British Commonwealth, thereby breaking traditions and established rules of loyalty and dependability. As things have turned out this now makes a change of government in Britain desirable in the national interest, not only for internal reasons but also from the point of view of its international relations, particularly with the Commonwealth.

The British application caused Denmark, Norway, and Ireland hurriedly to follow suit, and brought Sweden, Switzerland, and Austria to apply for associate membership.

And so the second act in the drama began which was to end early in 1963 with the collapse of the Brussels negotiations under circumstances which are too fresh in our memory to need to be recalled. Britain had been the only actor during this second act, while the others in E.F.T.A. had to remain in the wings, making appropriate, polite declarations of which nobody took any notice. "Je parle à mon bonnet," as one of their foreign ministers privately explained, quoting Molière.

To what extent American pressure had been effective in bringing Britain to change its position is not clear. What is certain, however, is that the United States government from the very beginning sided strongly with the Common Market and looked upon E.F.T.A. as a nuisance, if not a subversive force. Also during the negotiations in Brussels the United States used all the influence it had on all participating governments to get Britain into the Common Market.

The outcome was, therefore, undoubtedly an open rebuff for the United States as well. It was underlined by General de Gaulle's outspoken explanation, causing the Brussels negotiations to break up, that he looked upon Britain in the Common Market as an American agent. The United States had mixed into European affairs in a most conspicuous way, without having strength and influence enough to get its will accepted.

The fact that the French government so openly took the responsibility upon itself for this outcome made it easy for all the others to express regret and even anger. This concealed the fact that the French government was not as alone as it appeared in resisting the widening of membership in the Common Market. The Americans and, later, the British and the Scandinavians had been very outspoken in giving vent to the opinion that the whole character of the Common Market would change, once they had won entrance into it. The French made a *fait accompli,* and nobody else needed to act. There were more people in Little Europe than now needed to stand up and be counted who did not want themselves to be changed that way.

Undoubtedly, the dramatic break with the British—and the Americans who were so active in rounding them in— did add to the already existing tensions within the Common Market group of countries, and may contribute even in the future to hampering or delaying its further consolidation and, in particular, its development towards a political federation. With the unreserved position the United States government had taken toward such a development this will spell further reverses for its policy.

Quite aside from whether this policy was right, this is unfortunate from an American point of view. As I have pointed out already, influence is an expendable capital, and every time the United States goes strongly in for a policy without having the strength to see it through, its influence will by that outcome become even smaller than it need be. Influence, to be preserved, needs to be husbanded with utmost prudence. This the United States had obviously not done.

The Motives for the United States Policy

Looking into the reasons why the United States from the beginning took this position and finally incurred this rebuff, it is fairly clear that the political motive was the most important. This became further underlined by the

United States not wanting to have the neutral states—Sweden, Switzerland, and Austria—included in the widened Common Market.

The United States was in other words willing to pay the price of a common and, at least in the beginning, fairly stiff protective and discriminatory tariff wall built up against itself and the whole world in order to join more firmly together the West European countries belonging to NATO. This intention misfired. For it is now clear that the Brussels negotiations and their outcome instead aggravated the crisis in NATO and must contribute to making a solution of it that is satisfactory to the United States more difficult.

What has happened illustrates the danger of using economic means for purely political purposes. From an economic point of view, the policies of the countries belonging to E.F.T.A. are, of course, much more in line with the United States policy line in economic matters, particularly as this has been developed in recent years. That their national ethos and democratic institutions are also more similar has already been pointed out. E.F.T.A. as an international organization is less removed from the most-favored-nation clause which still is the bedrock of United States foreign commercial policy.

In particular, the supranational, bureaucratic, and undemocratic organization of the Common Market is entirely foreign to American conceptions. It can firmly be stated that no United States senator, living or dead, could ever have thought of permitting his country to join such an organization. How the United States could so lightheartedly have exerted pressure to get Britain which is so similar to the United States to do it remains a mystery.

The American public at large and, I am afraid, the Congress were left without full information about the constitution of the Common Market. They were also induced to take the view that the Common Market was the cause of the rapid and steady economic progress of the six countries that constitute its membership—or at least of the bigger of them, Germany, France, and Italy—with the implication that a widened membership would offer the same advantage to new members. This view is mistaken, as is proved in the professional economic literature. Their economic advance had started much earlier and has in fact now slowed down. The responsibility for misinforming the American people should not be placed only on the administration but must be shared by the expert participants in the public debate who either avoided these issues or sang in chorus with the official spokesmen. This is not healthy in a great democracy, proud of enjoying a government through discussion.

A more prudent policy on behalf of the United States, particularly as it should have known that its power to influence the outcome was no longer as great, would have been: to have recognized the rather fundamental differences in point of view of the two groups of countries, to have avoided prematurely taking a definite stand—and, in any case, not the one, which, it turned out, incurred a rebuff—and to have instead offered its good offices to induce the West European countries to co-operate as much as possible and in forms that were agreeable to both parties and to the United States.

When putting all its weight behind getting Britain to enter unconditionally into the continental organization, and the continental countries to receive Britain there, the United States not only invited defeat but forgot some of the main political facts in Europe. I think it needs to be stated that it is a doubtful philosophy to think of founding a democratic political federation in Europe with its center so definitely on the continent as the American scheme implied.

Of the three great powers on the continent, France is now under an authoritarian regime with great uncertainty as to the role that representative government is going to play in the future. West Germany is dismembered, is not at peace with the Soviet bloc, and officially still upholds irridentist claims that it has a right to territory on the other side of what they ominously call *Mittel-Deutschland,* *i.e.* the land east of the East German state. Italy is only emerging from a state in which political life was dominated by two basically totalitarian parties, the Vatican party, as it was until John XXIII, and the Communist party which still infiltrates economic and social activity like a huge Tammany organization. Stable democracy in Europe is to be found on the fringes, mainly outside the continent.

There is every reason to hope for a good development in the countries on the continent in the direction of the American ideals. And naturally, everybody wants to have a maximum of commerce and the friendliest relations with these countries in all other fields. Even a Swede can appreciate the United States' wish to have them as allies in the Cold War. But from this there is a big step to wanting to press for a European political federation having its center on the continent.

The Future

The second act ended in collapse and defeat. Unlike life on the stage, history does not know a finale, however, and a falling curtain. History goes on and on forever.

There is now a common tactical pattern in all West European countries (with the exception of France being reserved), as in the United States, not to take the breakup in Brussels as final but to insist that negotiations to widen the Common Market will soon be renewed and then be more successful. In the common interest of not aggravating the conflict, and since trade and all other relations must go on, this is diplomacy, which I do not criticize as diplomacy. But public opinion should not be misinformed. The people and the legislators have a right to see reality as it is. This must in any case be the scholar's concern. The ethos of his profession is that illusions are always dangerous, not least the opportunistic ones.

The present British government would have great difficulties in continuing to give up even as much as it had been prepared to give up under the pressure of the pending collapse of its policy to join the Common Market. It seems, moreover, probable that the present government will soon be out. It is certain that meanwhile it will have to tread most carefully on that very question. The Labour government, if and when it comes into power, is committed to go back on the compromises that were once conceded by the Tory government. That the Common Market countries on their side, in particular the French, should now be prepared to accept Britain on less favorable terms than they could have gotten before the breakup is inconceivable. The whole question of Britain's joining the Common Market has in reality been put on ice.

The initiative now passes to Britain and E.F.T.A. When the possibility of getting on terms with the Common Market on the basis of a widening of the latter organization proved illusory, it becomes all the more important that E.F.T.A.'s missed chance of turning to the outside world, to which I referred above, now finally be taken up in all seriousness.

In particular, the E.F.T.A. countries have an interest in getting the Common Market to lower its outer tariff wall. Such an attempt will be supported even within the Common Market itself where there are many forces working for a more outward-oriented commercial policy.

The United States shares in this interest. However the United States should realize that in the coming negotiations with the Common Market to be carried on under the auspices of G.A.T.T. it is not particularly strong if it should act alone.

Its tariffs are still high, even compared with the Common Market countries, and it has in relation to those countries a big export surplus. It needs allies.

The United States first needs the support of Britain. But it should be noted that, in its rather weak bargaining position, it even needs the Scandinavian countries in spite of their smallness. The latter countries, though having not more than a tenth of the population of the United States, import as much from the Common Market countries as the United States does. Sweden alone imports half as much from these countries as the United States.

The United States' exports, on the other hand, are more than twice as large as the Scandinavian countries' and almost four times the exports of Sweden. And while the United States has to plead for more open access of exports of wheat and poultry—against, in particular, strong French interests—Sweden is an exporter of industrial raw materials, such as wood products and iron ore, and in addition, products of high technology which even in the very last years have proven their competitive market strength and their power to climb over even fairly high tariff walls.

The United States, having failed to force a widening of the Common Market in Europe, is bound to pursue a policy of worldwide free trade among the rich countries more directly. When this policy line is clarified America will have to seek support from Britain, the other E.F.T.A. countries, from likeminded countries in the Common Market, and in the whole world.

For my own part, I am optimistic about the longer run. History now evolves so fast that the "long run" does not mean more than some years or a decade or two. If political and military events do not wreck the whole international political house of cards, I believe the rich countries will have to accept the responsibility of their advanced state and be prepared to move on their own towards freer trade, as Britain did a century ago when it was the only rich country, while at the same time accepting the right of the poor countries to protect their development and, even more, affording them a preferential treatment by the rich countries in their own markets. I have already pointed out that the ideological development in the United States has gone in this direction.

Bloc formation among the rich countries is an aberration from this natural and desirable course. Even the Common Market countries will in due course have to leave the protectionist road. They will, of course, still have open the possibility of consolidating economically and even of forming a political federation if they can, and they will then follow the constitutional and political patterns which are natural on the continent of Europe, though not in Britain and Scandinavia and, of course, not in the United States.

As tariffs come down everywhere, the countries in E.F.T.A. will have even fewer rational reasons to want to join the Common Market—which, of course, should not prevent some of them, and specifically Britain like the United States, from wanting to continue to be their political and military allies. With freer trade, and the recognized failure of the American attempt to force a shot-gun marriage sanctioned by a supranational bureaucracy, such a political and military alliance would, indeed, have a chance to develop with fewer internal tensions. This much we should learn from our recent experience.

The rapidity by which the development towards universal free trade for the rich countries with the right to protection for the underdeveloped countries, and even preferential treatment for their products in the markets of the former, will proceed, will depend very much on whether the United States is strong enough to supply a determined lead. The relative economic stagnation in the United States at present and its difficult foreign exchange situation have largely prevented that leadership from being forthcoming. These conditions have from time to time even caused the United States to take protectionist positions in questions of international trade in its own defense that are contrary to these principles. This, in its turn, has given encouragement and excuse to the protectionist forces in the Common Market and elsewhere.

There are reasons to fear that, in the absence of economic expansion at home, American leadership will remain particularly weak in the complex of problems concerning how the rich countries should frame their commercial and financial policies towards the underdeveloped countries. I have already stressed that much more important than "aid" is the way they are doing business with them.

The Trade Expansion Act is aimed mainly at freeing trade among the rich countries. No similarly dramatic challenge has been presented by the United States to stabilize the markets for traditional exports from the underdeveloped countries and still less to give them preferential treatment for exports of industrial products. On the contrary, the United States has joined, for instance, in pressing underdeveloped countries to accept limitations on their textile exports. If the American growth rate remains low and unemployment high and rising, there might be more such deviations from a fair treatment of poor countries. Indeed, under such conditions we might even see a more general retreat of American commercial policies towards old-fashioned protectionism.

A Main Conclusion

On many of the questions discussed above, there are possibilities of honest disagreement, and the debate will go on. I want only to retain one main conclusion which I believe is established and illustrated, namely that *whatever the United States foreign policy is or should be in various respects, it is highly important that its strength be recovered and retained.* That cannot be accomplished without a rapid and steady economic growth.

This is important both in order that its foreign policy should be considered in as calm and rational an atmosphere as possible and not be influenced by feelings of frustration and, of course, in order that the United States should have the influence and power to carry its policy through.

Even a strong America will always be limited in what it can achieve on the international scene. But it can also observe these limitations with greater equanimity because they will be wider, and can at the same time hope to be more effective within their bounds. At the present time there is a tendency that the United States, through its embassies in various countries and its representatives in international organizations, is trying to exert more and not less pressure on foreign governments to do, or not to do, this or that thing, than it did in the era of its strength. This is undoubtedly, in part at least, a result of frustration. And naturally it is not very successful. Even if in a particular matter it has its way, widespread irritation will remain a main result.

I have, as I said, a confident trust that a strong America will be a wiser America, less inclined to petty interventionism in other countries' affairs and, more important, less apt to run into policies that are ill-considered from the point of view of long-range goals and ideals and from the point of view of getting results and not leading to defeat.

Positively, I trust that a strong America will come to take leadership in the world for policies that are in the interests of liberty and equality on an international scale: free trade for the people in the rich countries, and protection and promotion for the many hundred millions of people in the huge world slum of the underdeveloped countries. A strong America is an open-minded, generous America and will now be wise enough to press other rich countries also to be open-minded and generous.

That America shall succeed in getting out of the rut of

slow economic progress while unemployment is high and rising is therefore in the interest of the world and not only of America. Indeed, as I see it, it is the most important problem in the world today.

APPENDIX

SINCE this address, focused on the problems of young Negro professionals, was written, and even since the writing of the manuscript of the rest of the book, the Negro protest has been rising and it has increasingly involved the broad masses of urban Negroes. The relative muteness of the American substratum, which is often referred to in this book, has for one group, the Negroes, almost changed into mutiny. I have to abstain from bringing this book up to date by taking up this development. Two remarks may, however, be made.

Even if this movement has been directed upon what can be broadly described as civil rights, it undoubtedly has its undertone and part of its momentum in the great poverty and high unemployment rate among the Negroes. In the constructive and courageous response to the movement by the present administration this is recognized.

The second remark is, that as yet there are no similar movements among other submerged groups on America.

Commencement Address

Ninety-fourth Annual Commencement,
Howard University, Washington, D.C.

June 8, 1962

I AM told that it is usual for commencement speakers to shape their remarks around the challenges which lie ahead for those of you who receive degrees today and who are about to leave the shelter of the university campus to take up your work and struggle in life. I do not normally pride myself on being a conformist. But there is, I believe, a special reason why this conventional pattern for commencement addresses is appropriate on this occasion. The challenges which face this generation of Howard University graduates are, I am certain, fundamentally different from those that confronted earlier generations of graduates. It is important to understand the nature of this difference, for it concerns not simply the future life of graduates from a single institution, but also the wider issue of the role of the Negro in American life.

The dimensions of the issue I have in mind can be understood most clearly if we first reflect for a moment on the circumstances which shaped Howard University and have given it a unique place in American higher education as the only university sponsored by the Federal Government. Born in the wake of the Civil War almost one hundred years ago, Howard was conceived as a Negro university and so it has largely remained. To an extent, there are still traces here of a segregation and discrimination in reverse, though, of course, the basic factor molding the composition of this university has been—and to a diminishing extent continues to be—restrictionism in various forms on the part of the majority group of white Americans who dominate the regular universities, particularly in the South. To this question I shall return in the course of my address.

When this university was founded, the United States had just emerged from the frightful agony of the most destructive and murderous war then known in human history. More than one million soldiers died. The costs, if we correct them for the different size and level of the American economy at that time, were staggering even from the point of view of today, when we have become so accustomed to spending astronomical sums on wars and on war preparation.

Even though this war undoubtedly had something to do with Negro slavery, it was not fought for the primary purpose of freeing Negroes. As often before and since, Negro people were more the pawns in a struggle between two camps of the dominant majority of white people who were fighting over quite different stakes. The Negroes themselves had practically no part in that struggle. Nevertheless, by the logic of events the abolition of slavery became the result of the exigencies of the Civil War.

When he took office in the Spring of 1861, Abraham Lincoln saw the preservation of the Union as the central issue and declared that he did not aim to take action against the institution of slavery in the states where it existed. But by the fall of 1862, the pressures of the war itself brought him to proclaim the abolition of slavery from the new year of 1863, though the coverage of this proclamation was then restricted to those states then in rebellion against the Government. It was not before the beginning of 1865 that Congress decided to free all slaves in the whole of the United States and not until the end of that year—when Lincoln was already dead—that the constitutional change was confirmed. And so the Negro people in America will now in the months and years to come have one important centennial after another to celebrate.

These were radical and far-reaching political changes. But as we can now look back over the era of Reconstruction with the wisdom of hindsight, we see clearly that the reason why so much went wrong and why so little permanent improvement of the lot of the Negroes in the South resulted was this: that the political revolution was not backed up by economic and social reform. As usual the leaders of that time tried to do great things too cheaply without paying the costs. The slogan "six acres and a mule" was never taken seriously by those in power— just as in most of the underdeveloped countries of the world today where land and tenancy reforms are proposed as programs and sometimes even enacted into law, but frustrated and nullified by the resistance of the vested interests. I draw this parallel between the fate of the Negro people in America during Reconstruction and that of the downtrodden masses in underdeveloped countries at the present time because I believe it has a lesson to teach us if we want to avert disaster. Today, too, a radical revolution has been carried out: the liquidation of colonial domination. But vicious economic and social systems, which colonial governments had found it to their advantage not to disturb, have largely been left intact; in some countries, inequalities are, in fact, increasing. Now history is repeating itself on a much bigger scale. It is not now a matter of a small minority of a few millions in one single country, as it was in post-Civil War time in America. Today huge majorities of many hundreds of millions in the greater part of the world outside the Soviet orbit are affected. The stage is international and not merely national, and the problems it presents are immensely dangerous in the present tense state of international relations, dominated by the Cold War.

In America this type of reconstruction led to the great national compromise worked out in the late 1870s. The

Negro people were left again to the mercy of the white upper caste in the South, now embittered by all that had followed their military defeat. Economically, the South deteriorated to a colonial status in its relation to the North, and as late as the thirties Franklin Roosevelt could still characterize the South as the nation's "problem number one." In the North there was instead huge immigration and economic expansion, though under "rugged individualism" and rampant corruption of government, from which America, as we know, has still not entirely freed itself.

Thereafter, for more than half a century—indeed, until the end of the thirties—the status of the Negro people remained on the whole about unchanged. There were advances on some fronts, but retreats on others. Twenty years ago this era of relative stagnation so far as the Negroes' position is concerned had so impressed itself on American thinking that even the social scientists had generally come to believe that it was the natural order of things. Progress was foredoomed to be very gradual and slow, they believed, and nothing very much could be done to speed it up. In my study of the Negro problem in America at that time, I came to the contrary conclusion, however, that this period of stagnation was only a temporary balancing of forces which was just on the verge of being broken. I saw big changes in the offing.

And, as we know, this actually happened. These last twenty years have been filled with advances on all fronts: in the labor market, in education, in the fields of social welfare and housing, in the structure of law and law observance, and generally in the enjoyment of more equal opportunities to do things, to move in society, to work, produce and consume without meeting segregation and discrimination. No historical trend of social change is a straight line, and there have been occasional setbacks. Prejudice itself is also slow to disappear, though its legal and institutional retaining walls are crumbling. There is still a long road to travel before America becomes in fact the egalitarian country of its creed. But in historical perspective the rapidity of progress is astonishing. Let us remember that practically all of this progress has taken place in the short period of the last twenty years, following six decades of stagnation—and that its coming was not anticipated by most students of the American scene.

I have found it not inappropriate to use this occasion for reminding us of some broad traits of the history of the Negro people over the past century. Just as an individual, for the sake of his sanity, needs to maintain continuity with his earliest memories, so also groups of people need to be clear about where they came from and how they have fared, if they are to understand where they stand today and the direction in which they are moving.

The progressive achievements of recent years have not been won without efforts. Every individual advance on the whole broad front has had to be fought for, sometimes against fierce resistance. In the general advance unfortunate incidents occur which deeply disturb the participants. But we should not expect the uprooting of racial inequality in the face of inherited and emotion-laden prejudices to be frictionless.

In a sense, unpleasant incidents even have a function to fulfill in this process of advance. In the last chapter of *An American Dilemma* I quoted a remark once made to me by a prominent and conservative Negro social scientist in the South; I can now reveal that the man I characterized in this way was my late friend Charles S. Johnson, the great sociologist and the first Negro president of Fisk University. He stated as his considered opinion that tensions are not necessarily bad and that under certain conditions even race riots may have wholesome effects in the long run. He continued in about the following way:

They stir up people's conscience. People will have to think matters over. They prevent things from becoming settled. If the race situation should ever become fixed, if the Negro were really accommodated, then, and only then, would I despair about a continued great improvement for Negroes. As long as there is friction and fighting, there is hope.

In this light, the Little Rock disturbances and the many other unfortunate incidents reported daily in the American press have their positive role to play in giving momentum to social advance. I realize that it is much easier for an outsider to take this lofty philosophical view than it is for the American citizen who has a duty to take a part in pressing social advance as rapidly as possible. And it must be particularly difficult for the young Negro intellectual who bears scars in his soul from all that yet remains of segregation and discrimination in American life. Nevertheless, I maintain that it is important to see clearly that the trend moves steeply upward, in order to avoid discouragement and to sustain the determination required in the skirmishing that may still be necessary. In this new epoch the Negro cause is a winning one.

I have not the slightest doubt that we shall continuously see great improvement in the Negro's status in American society, and I even foresee that the rising trend of the past two decades will accelerate. It would take me too far afield to explain all my reasons for this conviction. But among them, on the material side, is the higher productivity of society which should provide more elbow room for everybody and less interest in pushing anybody into the ditch. On the spiritual side, there is the reality of the ideals enshrined in your Constitution and rooted in the hearts of the American people. With rising levels of education the hold of these ideals in America is continuously strengthened. Increasingly, the false and derogatory beliefs about Negroes, which have filled the function of rationalizing prejudices, can be expressed only by those willing to betray their own lack of culture. As the white and Negro people are increasingly mingling in work and pleasure, all are discovering that they are the same sort of people with the same cultural moorings, the same likes and dislikes, and the same aspirations and ambitions for themselves and for America.

Just as until women are completely emancipated, every ambitious woman has also to stand for women's rights, so even today every Negro intellectual must feel called upon to supplement his work in his chosen vocation by being a "race man." This situation will remain until Negroes are generally accepted everywhere on a par with the whites. It is for this reason that we find my friend and former collaborator Ralph Bunche, who is working with so much distinction in the United Nations' peace-building efforts in the world, taking off time now and then to speak out for the Negroes. But increasingly the spokesmen for Negroes are finding that there are white people championing the same cause.

The changes now under way have important implications for the life all of you will be leading as you take up your careers and they will require more radical adjustments than earlier generations of Howard's graduates were called upon to make. What we shall see happening, and what has already happened to a considerable extent, is that the Negro intellectual increasingly steps out of his spiritual isolation and becomes simply an American amongst other Americans and a human being amongst us all. The Negro social scientist will less and less be preoccupied with research on the Negro community and will strike out in other and broader fields. The Negro doctor and dentist and lawyer will increasingly serve white patients and clients. This implies, however, that Negroes also will go to white doctors, dentists and lawyers. Similar changes in the activities of Negro clergymen and teachers can also be expected.

I should not be fully candid with you if at this point I did not stress another implication of the integration of the Negroes in the wider American society, namely that the Negro professional middle and upper class will have to surrender economic monopolies which they have held, and are still holding, on the basis of prejudice. The future society of equality is a society of free competition, and you will have to face it and prepare yourselves to deal with it successfully. You cannot cry for the breaking down of the walls of segregation and discrimination while, at the same time, hoping to retain petty monopoly preserves among a Negro clientele to give you a comfortable and uncontested economic safety. You must have the courage to choose a harder life in which your abilities will be tested against the norms established in the wider American society, and indeed, in the whole world. This is the point I should like to emphasize to the new graduates. A more egalitarian society is one offering vastly greater opportunities but also one which will subject you to tests far more severe than those set for your predecessors.

In the future America of our dreams, not only all schools, but also all institutions for higher education will stand open to all according to personal merit and independent of race and color. This will ultimately happen also in the South. In such an America there will be no place for a Negro university. I am, therefore, confidently looking forward to a day, even if it is not tomorrow, when Howard and Fisk and Atlanta Universities are not dissimilar in the composition of their faculties and student bodies from other universities in this country. This, of course, implies—and indeed requires as a condition—that all the other universities will have Negro professors and Negro students, as a normal thing. I am happy to know that even in this respect steady progress is being made in America, and that Howard University itself is increasingly opening its facilities for other young people than American Negroes—from America and from the whole world. Desegregation, even in regard to Howard University itself, is the declared policy of its administration. "My goal for Howard," said your President, Dr. Nabrit, "is to lead it into its new role as a major American university, into a normal society where a man is recognized for his own value and achievement."

As the integration process proceeds, the problems of the Negroes will gradually tend to disappear as separate problems. For a long time yet, there will undoubtedly be problems of breaking down segregation and discrimination against Negro families in housing. But the general problem of slum clearance in American cities is the bigger and more important one. And the Negro's stake in that bigger problem is the greater as there is no hope for a satisfactory separate solution to the housing problems of Negroes as long as slums remain a blot on American cities. The schools most Negro children attend are bad in the South and often in some parts of the North, but many other schools are also bad, and the best hope for Negroes, particularly in this period of desegregation, is a campaign for improving the schools generally. Likewise, Negroes, as members of the group still most disadvantaged in American society, have a particular interest in the extension of social security, an area in which America is still rather backward (particularly in the field of health and hospitalization) by comparison with the most advanced countries. In this situation, it is both natural and necessary that Negroes should support and join those forces in American society which stand for general social and economic progress. When narrower group interests are submerged and the pursuit of social advance for the whole community is brought to the fore, a major step toward the complete integration of Negroes in American society will have been taken.

It probably still is broadly true, though less now than twenty or thirty years ago, that the Negroes are the "last hired and the first fired," and the incidence of unemployment of Negro workers is disproportionally heavy. The state of full employment, created by the war and preserved in the immediate postwar years, was of great importance on the economic side in supporting the rising trend in the Negro's status. The relative economic stagnation in America and the high unemployment since the fifties is, for the same reason, particularly menacing for Negro advance. If continued stagnation should be the lasting condition for the American economy in the decades to come, it will for America spell frustration internally and externally, and it might even slow down the upward trend of Negro advance I have talked about. When I have expressed my faith that the trend to improvement of the Negroes' status will continue and indeed gather momentum, I have done so because I cannot believe that the American people will tolerate a stagnating economy for much longer. It is not necessary. Any economist worth his salt can tell you what is needed in the field of public policy to make America a country of bold and rapid economic progress.

To fight discrimination against Negroes in the labor market remains naturally a task that cannot be relaxed. But much more important is the creation of the conditions for American economic progress, as nothing is more effective in liquidating discrimination than full employment and a rising trend of incomes to all.

In this way, the cause of raising the status of the Negroes in America and stamping out the remnants of segregation and discrimination is bound up more closely than ever before with all the progressive causes in the country. As American Negroes you have no reason to have a split personality. The integration of the Negroes in American society has already proceeded so far that without any hesitation you can feel that what is good for America is good for the Negroes—and equally you can feel that what is good for the Negroes is good for America. The graduates who today leave Howard University are in that respect far better favored than were their parents and grandparents.